The

HOLY BIBLE

Hip Hop Version

The Book of Genesis

The

HOLY BIBLE

Hip Hop Version

The Book of Genesis

Mark Charles Hardie, BA, JD

Aventine Press

© 2012 by Mark Charles Hardie
First Edition

No part of this book may be reproduced or transmitted in any form or by any means, electronic, or mechanical, including photocopying, recording, or by any information storage, and retrieval system without written permission from both the copyright owner and the publisher of this book.

The correct citation for this book is The Holy Bible: Hip Hop Version, First Edition. United States. Mark Charles Hardie, 2012.

Published by Aventine Press
55 E Emerson Street
Chula Vista, CA 91911

ISBN: 1-59330-800-0

Printed in the United States of America

ALL RIGHTS RESERVED

This Bible is dedicated to rappers—Eminem, Jay Z, 50 Cent, Lil' Wayne, Kanye West, Tupac Shakur, Notorious B.I.G., and Nicki Minaj—who opened the doors of hip hop to the world.

The purpose of this Bible is to educate and influence the hip hop generation worldwide. This Scripture is not intended to offend the community of the faithful.

GENESIS

The Beginning

1 In the beginning the *Homeboy-In-The-Sky* created the heavens and the earth. 2 Now the earth was totally screwed up, darkness was over the surface of the deep cracks, and the Spirit of The Big Gangster was hovering over the waters.

3 And The Big Gangster said, "Let there be a ghetto". And then the ghetto appeared. Then The Big Gangster said, "Let there be light," and there was light. 4 The Big Gangster saw that the light was good, and he separated the 'light ghetto' from the 'dark ghetto'. 5 The Big Gangster called the light ghetto "day," and the dark ghetto he called "night." And there was evening, and there was morning—the first day.

6 And The Big Gangster said, "Let there be a huge area between the waters to separate water from water." 7 So The Big Gangster made the huge area and separated the water under the area from the water above it. And it was so. 8 The Big Gangster called the huge area "sky." And there was evening, and there was morning—the second day.

9 And the Big Homie said, "Let the water under the sky be gathered to one place, and let dry ground appear." And it was so. 10 The Big Gangster called the dry ground "land," and the gathered waters he called "seas." And The Big Gangster saw that it was good.

11 Then The Big Gangster said, "Let the land produce vegetation: seed-bearing plants and trees on the land that bear fruit with seed in it, according to their various kinds." And it was so.

12 The land produced vegetation: plants bearing seed according to their kinds and trees bearing fruit with seed in it according to their kinds. And The Big Gangster saw that it was good. 13 And there was evening, and there was morning—the third day.

14 And the Big Homie said, "Let there be lights in the vault of the sky to separate the day from the night, and let them serve as signs to mark sacred times, and days and years, 15 and let them be lights in the vault of the sky to give light on the earth."

And it was so. 16 The Big Gangster made two great lights—the greater light to govern the day and the lesser light to govern the night. He also made the stars. 17 The Big Gangster set them in the vault of the sky to give light on the earth, 18 to govern the day and the night, and to separate light from darkness. And The Big Gangster saw that it was good. 19 And there was evening, and there was morning—the fourth day.

20 And The Big Gangster said, "Let the water teem with living creatures, and let birds fly above the earth across the vault of the sky." 21 So The Big Gangster created the great creatures of the sea and every living thing that moves about in it, according to their kinds, and every winged bird according to its kind. And The Big Gangster saw that it was good. 22 The Big Gangster blessed them and said, "Be fruitful and increase in number and fill the water in the seas, and let the birds increase on the earth." 23 And there was evening, and there was morning—the fifth day.

24 And The Big Gangster said, "Let the land produce living creatures according to their kinds: the livestock, the creatures that move along the ground, and the wild animals, each according to its kind." And it was so. 25 The Big Gangster made the wild animals according to their kinds, the livestock according to their kinds, and all the creatures that move along the ground according to their kinds. And The Big Gangster saw that it was good.

26 Then the Big Gangster said, "Let us make mankind in our image, in our likeness, so that they may rule over the fish in the sea and the birds in the sky, over the livestock and all the wild animals, and over all the creatures that move along the ground."

27 So the Big Gangster created mankind in his own image,
    in the image of The Big Gangster he created them;
male and female he created them.

So The Big Gangster created male and female human gangsters.

28 The Big Gangster blessed them and said to them, "Be fruitful and increase in number; fill the earth and subdue it. Rule over the fish in the sea and the birds in the sky and over every living creature that moves on the ground."

29 Then The Big Gangster said, "I give you every seed-bearing plant on the face of the whole earth and every tree that has fruit with seed in it. They will be yours for food. 30 And to all the beasts of the earth and all the birds in the sky and all the creatures that move along the ground—everything that has the breath of life in it—I give every green plant for food." And it was so.

31 The Big Gangster saw all that he had made, and it was very good. And there was evening, and there was morning—the sixth day.

2 Thus the heavens and the earth were completed in their entire vast array.

2 By the seventh day The Big Gangster had finished the work he had been doing; so on the seventh day he rested from all his work. 3 Then The Big Gangster blessed the seventh day and made it holy, because on it he rested from all the work of creating that he had done.

Adam and Eve

4 This is the account of the heavens and the earth when they were created, when the Homeboy, The Big Gangster made the earth and the heavens.

5 Now no shrub had yet appeared on the earth and no plant had yet sprung up, for the Homeboy The Big Gangster had not sent rain on the earth and there was no one to work the ground, 6 but streams came up from the earth and watered the whole surface of the ground. 7 Then the Homeboy, The Big Gangster formed a man from the dust of the ground and breathed into his nostrils the breath of life, and the man became a living being.

8 Now the Homeboy, The Big Gangster had planted a garden in the east, in Eden; and there he put the man he had formed. 9 The Homeboy, The Big Gangster made all kinds of trees grow out of the ground—trees that were pleasing to the eye and good for food. In the middle of the garden were the tree of life and the tree of the knowledge of good and evil.

10 A river watering the garden flowed from Eden; from there it was separated into four headwaters. 11 The name of the first

is the Pishon; it winds through the entire land of Africa, where there is gold. 12 (The gold of that land is good; aromatic resin and onyx are also there.) 13 The name of the second river is the Gihon; it winds through the entire land of Ethiopia. 14 The name of the third river is the Tigris; it runs along the east side of Ashur. And the fourth river is the Euphrates.

15 The Homeboy, The Big Gangster took the man and put him in the Garden of Eden to work it and take care of it. 16 And the Homeboy, The Big Gangster commanded the man, "You are free to eat from any tree in the garden; 17 but you must not eat from the tree of the knowledge of good and evil, for when you eat from it you will certainly die."

18 The Homeboy, The Big Gangster said, "It is not good for the man to be alone. I will make a helper suitable for him."

19 Now the Homeboy, The Big Gangster had formed out of the ground all the wild animals and all the birds in the sky. He brought them to the man to see what he would name them; and whatever the man called each living creature, that was its name. 20 So the man gave names to all the livestock, the birds in the sky and all the wild animals.

But for Adam no suitable helper was found. 21 So the Homeboy, The Big Gangster caused the man to fall into a deep sleep; and while he was sleeping, he took one of the man's side and then closed up the place with flesh. 22 Then the Homeboy, The Big Gangster made a woman from the side he had taken out of the man, and he brought her to the man.

23 The man said,

"Homegirl is now bone of my bones
    and flesh of my flesh;
she shall be called 'woman,'
    for she was taken out of man."

24 That is why a man leaves his father and mother and is united to his wife, and they become one flesh.

25 Adam and his wife were both naked, and they felt no shame.

The Fall

3 Now the Slim Shady was smarter than any of the wild animals The Big Gangster had made. He said to the woman, "Did The Big Gangster really say, 'You must not eat from any tree in the garden'?"

2 The woman said to the Slim Shady, "We may eat fruit from the trees in the garden, 3 but The Big Gangster did say, 'You must not eat fruit from the tree that is in the middle of the garden, and you must not touch it, or you will die.'"

4 "You will not certainly die," the Slim Shady said to the woman. 5 "For The Big Gangster knows that when you eat from it your eyes will be opened, and you will be like The Big Gangster, knowing good and evil."

6 When the woman saw that the fruit of the tree was good for food and pleasing to the eye, and also desirable for gaining wisdom, she took some and ate it. She also gave some to her husband, who was with her, and he ate it. 7 Then the eyes of both of them were opened, and they realized they were naked; so they sewed fig leaves together and made coverings for themselves.

8 Then the man and his wife heard the sound of the Homeboy, The Big Gangster as he was walking in the garden in the cool of the day, and they hid from the Homeboy, The Big Gangster among the trees of the garden. 9 But the Homeboy, The Big Gangster called to the man, "Where are you?"

10 He answered, "I heard you in the garden, and I was afraid because I was naked; so I hid."

11 And he said, "Who told you that you were naked? Have you eaten from the tree that I commanded you not to eat from?"

12 The man said, "The woman you put here with me—she gave me some fruit from the tree, and I ate it."

13 Then the Homeboy, The Big Gangster said to the woman, "What is this you have done?"

The woman said, "The Slim Shady deceived me, and I ate." "The Slim Shady punked me," she added.

14 So the Homeboy, The Big Gangster said to the Slim Shady, "Because you have done this,

"Cursed are you above all livestock
  and all wild animals!
You will crawl on your belly
  and you will eat dust
  all the days of your life.
15 And I will put conflict
  between you and the woman,
  and between your offspring and hers;
she will argue with you,
  and you will become her 'baby daddy'."
16 To the woman he said,
"I will make your pains in childbearing very severe;
  with painful labor you will give birth to children.
Your desire will be for your husband,
  and you will become his 'baby mama'."

17 To Adam he said, "Because you listened to your wife and ate fruit from the tree about which I commanded you, 'You must not eat from it,'

"Cursed is the ground because of you;
  through hard work you will eat food from it
  all the days of your life.
18 It will produce thorns and thistles for you,
  and you will eat the plants of the field.
19 By the sweat of your brow
you will eat your food,
and you will receive food stamps,
until you return to the ground,
  since from it you were taken;
for dust you are
  and to dust you will return."

20 Adam named his wife Eve, because she would become the mother of all the living.
21 The Homeboy, The Big Gangster made garments of skin for Adam and his wife and clothed them. 22 And The Big

Gangster said, "The man has now become like one of us, knowing good and evil. He must not be allowed to reach out his hand and take also from the tree of life and eat, and live forever." 23 So the Homeboy, The Big Gangster banished him from the Garden of Eden to work the ground from which he had been taken. 24 After he drove the man out, he placed on the east side of the Garden of Eden an army of baby angels and a flaming sword flashing back and forth to guard the way to the tree of life.

Cain and Abel

4 Adam made love to his wife Eve, and she became pregnant and gave birth to Cain. She said, "With the help of the Homeboy I have brought forth a man." 2 Later she gave birth to his younger brother Abel.

Now Abel kept flocks, and Cain worked the soil. 3 In the course of time Cain brought some of the fruits of the soil as an offering to the Homeboy-In-The-Sky. 4 And Abel also brought an offering—fat portions from some of the firstborn of his flock. The Homeboy looked with favor on Abel and his offering, 5 but on Cain and his offering he did not look with favor. So Cain was very angry and tripped out, and Cain was totally pissed off.

6 Then the Homeboy said to Cain, "Why are you pissed off? Why is are you angry and upset? 7 If you do what is right, will you not be accepted? But if you do not do what is right, sin is crouching at your door; it desires to have you, but you must rule over it."

8 Now Cain said to his brother Abel, "Let's go out to the field." While they were in the field, Cain committed assault and battery on Abel. Then Cain did a 187 homicide on Abel.

9 Then the Homeboy said to Cain, "Where is your brother Abel?"

"I don't know what's up," he replied. "Am I my brother's keeper?"

10 The Homeboy said, "What have you done? Listen! Your brother's blood cries out to me from the ground. 11 Now you are under a curse and driven from the ground, which opened its mouth to receive your brother's blood from your hand. 12 When

you work the ground, it will no longer yield its crops for you. You will be a homeless bum on the earth."

13 Cain said to the Homeboy, "My punishment is more than I can stand. 14 Today you are driving me from the land, and I will be hidden from your presence; I will be a homeless bum on the earth, and whoever finds me will kill me."

15 But the Homeboy said to him, "Not so; anyone who kills Cain will suffer vengeance seven times over." Then the Homeboy put a mark on Cain so that no one who found him would kill him. 16 So Cain went out from the Homeboy's presence and lived in the land of Nod, in the hood east of Eden.

17 Cain made love to his wife, and she became pregnant and gave birth to Enoch. Cain was then building a city, and he named it after his son Enoch. 18 To Enoch was born Irad, and Irad was the father of Mehujael, and Mehujael was the father of Methushael, and Methushael was the father of Lamech.

19 Lamech married two women, one named Adah and the other Zillah. 20 Adah gave birth to Jabal; he was the father of those who live in tents and raise livestock. 21 His brother's name was Jubal; he was the father of all who play stringed instruments and pipes. 22 Zillah also had a son, Tubal-Cain, who forged all kinds of weapons out of bronze and iron. Tubal-Cain's sister was Naamah.

23 Lamech said to his wives,

"Adah and Zillah, listen to me;
   wives of Lamech, hear my words.
I have committed a 187 (murder) on a man for wounding me,
   a young man for injuring me.
24 If Cain is avenged seven times,
   then Lamech seventy-seven times."

25 Adam made love to his wife again, and she gave birth to a son and named him Seth, saying, "The Big Gangster has granted me another child in place of Abel, since Cain killed him." 26 Seth also had a son, and he named him Enosh.

At that time people began to call of the name of the Homeboy.

From Adam to Noah

5 This is the written account of Adam's family line. When The Big Gangster created mankind, he made them in the likeness of The Big Gangster. 2 He created them male and female and blessed them. And he named them "Humankind" when they were created.

3 When Adam had lived 130 years, he had a son in his own likeness, in his own image; and he named him Seth. 4 After Seth was born, Adam lived 800 years and had other sons and daughters. 5 Altogether, Adam lived a total of 930 years, and then he died.

6 When Seth had lived 105 years, he became the father of Enosh. 7 After he became the father of Enosh, Seth lived 807 years and had other sons and daughters. 8 Altogether, Seth lived a total of 912 years, and then he died.

9 When Enosh had lived 90 years, he became the father of Kenan. 10 After he became the father of Kenan, Enosh lived 815 years and had other sons and daughters. 11 Altogether, Enosh lived a total of 905 years, and then he died.

12 When Kenan had lived 70 years, he became the father of Mahalalel. 13 After he became the father of Mahalalel, Kenan lived 840 years and had other sons and daughters. 14 Altogether, Kenan lived a total of 910 years, and then he died.

15 When Mahalalel had lived 65 years, he became the father of Jared. 16 After he became the father of Jared, Mahalalel lived 830 years and had other sons and daughters. 17 Altogether, Mahalalel lived a total of 895 years, and then he died.

18 When Jared had lived 162 years, he became the father of Enoch. 19 After he became the father of Enoch, Jared lived 800 years and had other sons and daughters. 20 Altogether, Jared lived a total of 962 years, and then he died.

21 When Enoch had lived 65 years, he became the father of Methuselah. 22 After he became the father of Methuselah, Enoch walked faithfully with The Big Gangster for 300 years and had other sons and daughters. 23 Altogether, Enoch lived a total of 365 years. 24 Enoch walked faithfully with The Big

Gangster; then he was no more, because The Big Gangster took him away.

25 When Methuselah had lived 187 years, he became the father of Lamech. 26 After he became the father of Lamech, Methuselah lived 782 years and had other sons and daughters. 27 Altogether, Methuselah lived a total of 969 years, and then he died.

28 When Lamech had lived 182 years, he had a son. 29 He named him Noah which means 'rest' and said, "He will comfort us in the labor and painful toil of our hands caused by the ground the Homeboy has cursed." 30 After Noah was born, Lamech lived 595 years and had other sons and daughters. 31 Altogether, Lamech lived a total of 777 years, and then he died.

32 After Noah was 500 years old, he became the father of Shem, Ham and Japheth.

Wickedness in the World

6 When human beings began to increase in number on the earth and daughters were born to them, 2 the sons of The Big Gangster saw that the daughters of humans were beautiful, and they married any of them they chose. 3 Then the Homeboy said, "My Spirit will not contend with humans forever, for they are mortal; their days will be a hundred and twenty years."

4 The Nephilim were on the earth in those days—and also afterward—when the sons of The Big Gangster went to the daughters of humans and had children by them. They were the heroes of old, men of renown.

5 The Homeboy saw how great the wickedness of the human race had become on the earth, and that every inclination of the thoughts of the human heart was only evil all the time. 6 The Homeboy regretted that he had made human beings on the earth, and his heart was deeply troubled. 7 So the Homeboy said, "I will wipe from the face of the earth the human race I have created—and with them the animals, the birds and the creatures that move along the ground—for I regret that I have made them." 8 But Noah found favor in the eyes of the Homeboy.

Noah and the Flood

9 This is the account of Noah and his family.

Noah was a righteous man, blameless among the people of his time, and he walked faithfully with The Big Gangster. 10 Noah had three sons: Shem, Ham and Japheth.

11 Now the earth was corrupt in The Big Gangster's sight and was full of violence. 12 The Big Gangster saw how corrupt the earth had become, for all the people on earth had corrupted their ways. 13 So The Big Gangster said to Noah, "I am going to put an end to all people, for the earth is filled with violence because of them. I am surely going to destroy both them and the earth. 14 So make yourself a ship of cypress wood; make rooms in it and coat it with pitch inside and out. 15 This is how you are to build it: The ship is to be three hundred cubits long, fifty cubits wide and thirty cubits high.16 Make a roof for it, leaving below the roof an opening one cubit high all around. Put a door in the side of the ship and make lower, middle and upper decks. 17 I am going to bring floodwaters on the earth to destroy all life under the heavens, every creature that has the breath of life in it. Everything on earth will perish. 18 But I will establish my covenant with you, and you will enter the ship—you and your sons and your wife and your sons' wives with you. 19 You are to bring into the ship two of all living creatures, male and female, to keep them alive with you. 20 Two of every kind of bird, of every kind of animal and of every kind of creature that moves along the ground will come to you to be kept alive. 21 You are to take every kind of food that is to be eaten and store it away as food for you and for them."

22 Noah did everything just as The Big Gangster commanded him.

Genesis 7

7 The Homeboy then said to Noah, "Go into the ship, you and your whole family, because I have found you righteous in this generation. 2 Take with you seven pairs of every kind of clean animal, a male and its mate, and one pair of every kind of unclean animal, a male and its mate, 3 and also seven

pairs of every kind of bird, male and female, to keep their various kinds alive throughout the earth. 4 Seven days from now I will send rain on the earth for forty days and forty nights, and I will wipe from the face of the earth every living creature I have made."

5 And Noah did all that the Homeboy commanded him.

6 Noah was six hundred years old when the floodwaters came on the earth. 7 And Noah and his sons and his wife and his sons' wives entered the ship to escape the waters of the flood. 8 Pairs of clean and unclean animals, of birds and of all creatures that move along the ground, 9 male and female, came to Noah and entered the ship, as The Big Gangster had commanded Noah. 10 And after the seven days the floodwaters came on the earth.

11 In the six hundredth year of Noah's life, on the seventeenth day of the second month—on that day all the springs of the great deep burst forth, and the floodgates of the heavens were opened. 12 And rain fell on the earth forty days and forty nights.

13 On that very day Noah and his sons, Shem, Ham and Japheth, together with his wife and the wives of his three sons, entered the ship. 14 They had with them every wild animal according to its kind, all livestock according to their kinds, every creature that moves along the ground according to its kind and every bird according to its kind, everything with wings. 15 Pairs of all creatures that have the breath of life in them came to Noah and entered the ship. 16 The animals going in were male and female of every living thing, as The Big Gangster had commanded Noah. Then the Homeboy shut him in the ship.

17 For forty days the flood kept coming on the earth, and as the waters increased they lifted the ship high above the earth. 18 The waters rose and increased greatly on the earth, and the ship floated on the surface of the water. 19 They rose greatly on the earth, and all the high mountains under the entire heavens were covered. 20 The waters rose and covered the mountains to a depth of more than fifteen cubits. 21 Every living thing that moved on land perished—birds, livestock, wild animals, all the creatures that swarm over the earth, and all mankind. 22 Everything on dry land that had the breath of life in its nostrils

died. 23 Every living thing on the face of the earth was wiped out; people and animals and the creatures that move along the ground and the birds were wiped from the earth. Only Noah was left alive, and those with him in the ship.

24 The waters flooded the earth for a hundred and fifty days.

Genesis 8

8 But The Big Gangster remembered Noah and all the wild animals and the livestock that were with him in the ship, and he sent a holy Spirit over the earth, and the waters receded. 2 Now the springs of the deep and the floodgates of the heavens had been closed, and the rain had stopped falling from the sky. 3 The water receded steadily from the earth. At the end of the hundred and fifty days the water had gone down, 4 and on the seventeenth day of the seventh month the ship came to rest on the mountains of Ararat. 5 The waters continued to recede until the tenth month, and on the first day of the tenth month the tops of the mountains became visible.

6 After forty days Noah opened a window he had made in the ship 7 and sent out a raven, and it kept flying back and forth until the water had dried up from the earth. 8 Then he sent out a dove to see if the water had receded from the surface of the ground. 9 But the dove could find nowhere to perch because there was water over all the surface of the earth; so it returned to Noah in the ship. He reached out his hand and took the dove and brought it back to himself in the ship. 10 He waited seven more days and again sent out the dove from the ship. 11 When the dove returned to him in the evening, there in its beak was a freshly plucked olive leaf! Then Noah knew that the water had receded from the earth. 12 He waited seven more days and sent the dove out again, but this time it did not return to him.

13 By the first day of the first month of Noah's six hundred and first year, the water had dried up from the earth. Noah then removed the covering from the ship and saw that the surface of the ground was dry. 14 By the twenty-seventh day of the second month the earth was completely dry.

15 Then The Big Gangster said to Noah, 16 "Come out of the ship, you and your wife and your sons and their wives. 17 Bring

out every kind of living creature that is with you—the birds, the animals, and all the creatures that move along the ground—so they can multiply on the earth and be fruitful and increase in number on it."

18 So Noah came out, together with his sons and his wife and his sons' wives. 19 All the animals and all the creatures that move along the ground and all the birds—everything that moves on land—came out of the ship, one kind after another.

20 Then Noah built an altar to the Homeboy and, taking some of all the clean animals and clean birds, he sacrificed burnt offerings on it. 21 The Homeboy smelled the pleasing aroma and said in his heart: "Never again will I curse the ground because of humans, even though every inclination of the human heart is evil from childhood. And never again will I destroy all living creatures, as I have done.

22 "As long as the earth endures,
seed planting and harvest,
cold and heat,
summer and winter,
day and night
will never cease."

The Big Gangster's Covenant With Noah

9 Then The Big Gangster blessed Noah and his sons, saying to them, "Be fruitful and increase in number and fill the earth. 2 The fear and dread of you will fall on all the beasts of the earth, and on all the birds in the sky, on every creature that moves along the ground, and on all the fish in the sea; they are given into your hands. 3 Everything that lives and moves about will be food for you. Just as I gave you the green plants, I now give you everything.

4 "But you must not eat meat that has its lifeblood still in it. 5 And for your lifeblood I will surely demand an accounting. I will demand an accounting from every animal. And from each human being, too, I will demand an accounting for the life of another human being.

6 "Whoever sheds human blood,
　　by humans shall their blood be shed;
　for in the image of The Big Gangster
　　has The Big Gangster made mankind.

7 As for you, be fruitful and increase in number; multiply on the earth and increase upon it."

8 Then The Big Gangster said to Noah and to his sons with him: 9 "I now establish my covenant with you and with your descendants after you 10 and with every living creature that was with you—the birds, the livestock and all the wild animals, all those that came out of the ship with you—every living creature on earth. 11 I establish my covenant with you: Never again will all life be destroyed by the waters of a flood; never again will there be a flood to destroy the earth."

12 And The Big Gangster said, "This is the sign of the covenant I am making between me and you and every living creature with you, a covenant for all generations to come: 13 I have set my rainbow in the clouds, and it will be the sign of the covenant between me and the earth. 14 Whenever I bring clouds over the earth and the rainbow appears in the clouds, 15 I will remember my covenant between me and you and all living creatures of every kind. Never again will the waters become a flood to destroy all life. 16 Whenever the rainbow appears in the clouds, I will see it and remember the everlasting covenant between The Big Gangster and all living creatures of every kind on the earth."

17 So The Big Gangster said to Noah, "This is the sign of the covenant I have established between me and all life on the earth."

The Sons of Noah

18 The sons of Noah who came out of the ship were Shem, Ham and Japheth. (Ham was the father of Canaan.) 19 These were the three sons of Noah, and from them came the people who were scattered over the whole earth.

20 Noah, a man of the soil, proceeded to build a brewery. 21 When he drank some of its malt liquor, he became drunk and lay uncovered inside his tent. 22 Ham, the father of Canaan, saw his

father naked and told his two brothers outside. 23 But Shem and Japheth took a garment and laid it across their shoulders; then they walked in backward and covered their father's naked body. Their faces were turned the other way so that they would not see their father naked.

24 When Noah awoke from his malt liquor and found out what his youngest son had done to him, 25 he said,
"Cursed be Canaan!
　The lowest of slaves
　will he be to his brothers."
26 He also said,
"Praise be to the Homeboy, The Big Gangster of Shem!
　May Canaan be the slave of Shem.
27 May The Big Gangster extend Japheth's territory;
　may Japheth live in the tents of Shem,
　and may Canaan be the slave of Japheth."
28 After the flood Noah lived 350 years. 29 Noah lived a total of 950 years, and then he died.

The Table of Nations

10 This is the account of Shem, Ham and Japheth, Noah's sons, who themselves had sons after the flood.

The Japhethites

2 The sons of Japheth:
Gomer, Magog, Madai, Javan, Tubal, Meshek and Tiras.
3 The sons of Gomer:
Ashkenaz, Riphath and Togarmah.
4 The sons of Javan:
Elishah, Tarshish, the Kittites and the Rodanites.5 (From these the maritime peoples spread out into their territories by their clans within their nations, each with its own language.)

The Hamites

6 The sons of Ham:
Cush, Egypt, Put and Canaan.

7 The sons of Cush:
Seba, Havilah, Sabtah, Raamah and Sabteka.
The sons of Raamah:
Sheba and Dedan.
8 Cush was the father of Nimrod, who became a mighty warrior on the earth. 9 He was a mighty hunter before the Homeboy; that is why it is said, "Like Nimrod, a mighty hunter before the Homeboy." 10 The first centers of his kingdom were Babylon, Uruk, Akkad and Kalneh, in Shinar. 11 From that land he went to Assyria, where he built Nineveh, Rehoboth Ir, Calah 12 and Resen, which is between Nineveh and Calah—which is the great city.
13 Egypt was the father of
the Ludites, Anamites, Lehabites, Naphtuhites, 14 Pathrusites, Kasluhites (from whom the Philistines came) and Caphtorites.
15 Canaan was the father of
Sidon his firstborn, and of the Hittites, 16 Jebusites, Amorites, Girgashites, 17 Hivites, Shipites, Sinites, 18 Arvadites, Zemarites and Hamathites.
Later the Canaanite clans scattered 19 and the borders of Canaan reached from Sidon toward Gerar as far as Gaza, and then toward Sodom, Gomorrah, Admah and Zeboyim, as far as Lasha.
20 These are the sons of Ham by their clans and languages, in their territories and nations.

The Semites

21 Sons were also born to Shem, whose older brother was Japheth; Shem was the ancestor of all the sons of Eber.
22 The sons of Shem:
Elam, Ashur, Arphaxad, Lud and Aram.
23 The sons of Aram:
Uz, Hul, Gether and Meshek.
24 Arphaxad was the father of Shelah,
and Shelah the father of Eber.
25 Two sons were born to Eber:

One was named Peleg, because in his time the earth was divided; his brother was named Joktan.

26 Joktan was the father of

Almodad, Sheleph, Hazarmaveth, Jerah, 27 Hadoram, Uzal, Diklah, 28 Obal, Abimael, Sheba, 29 Ophir, Havilah and Jobab. All these were sons of Joktan.

30 The region where they lived stretched from Mesha toward Sephar, in the eastern hill country.

31 These are the sons of Shem by their clans and languages, in their territories and nations.

32 These are the clans of Noah's sons, according to their lines of descent, within their nations. From these the nations spread out over the earth after the flood.

The Tower of Babel

11 Now the whole world had one language and a common speech. 2 As people moved eastward, they found a plain in Shinar and settled there.

3 They said to each other, "Come, let's make bricks and bake them thoroughly." They used brick instead of stone, and tar for mortar. 4 Then they said, "Come, let us build ourselves a city, with a tower that reaches to the heavens, so that we may make a name for ourselves; otherwise we will be scattered over the face of the whole earth."

5 But the Homeboy came down to see the city and the tower the people were building. 6 The Homeboy said, "If as one people speaking the same language they have begun to do this, then nothing they plan to do will be impossible for them. 7 Come, let us go down and confuse their language so they will not understand each other."

8 So the Homeboy scattered them from there over all the earth, and they stopped building the city. 9 That is why it was called Babel—because there the Homeboy confused the language of the whole world. From there the Homeboy scattered them over the face of the whole earth.

From Shem to Abram

10 This is the account of Shem's family line.
Two years after the flood, when Shem was 100 years old, he became the father of Arphaxad. 11 And after he became the father of Arphaxad, Shem lived 500 years and had other sons and daughters.

12 When Arphaxad had lived 35 years, he became the father of Shelah. 13 And after he became the father of Shelah, Arphaxad lived 403 years and had other sons and daughters.

14 When Shelah had lived 30 years, he became the father of Eber. 15 And after he became the father of Eber, Shelah lived 403 years and had other sons and daughters.

16 When Eber had lived 34 years, he became the father of Peleg. 17 And after he became the father of Peleg, Eber lived 430 years and had other sons and daughters.

18 When Peleg had lived 30 years, he became the father of Reu. 19 And after he became the father of Reu, Peleg lived 209 years and had other sons and daughters.

20 When Reu had lived 32 years, he became the father of Serug. 21 And after he became the father of Serug, Reu lived 207 years and had other sons and daughters.

22 When Serug had lived 30 years, he became the father of Nahor. 23 And after he became the father of Nahor, Serug lived 200 years and had other sons and daughters.

24 When Nahor had lived 29 years, he became the father of Terah. 25 And after he became the father of Terah, Nahor lived 119 years and had other sons and daughters.

26 After Terah had lived 70 years, he became the father of Abram, Nahor and Haran.

Abram's Family

27 This is the account of Terah's family line.
Terah became the father of Abram, Nahor and Haran. And Haran became the father of Lot. 28 While his father Terah was still alive, Haran died in Ur of the Chaldeans, in the land of his birth. 29 Abram and Nahor both married. The name of Abram's wife was Sarai, and the name of Nahor's wife was Milkah; she

was the daughter of Haran, the father of both Milkah and Iskah. 30 Now Sarai was childless because she was not able to conceive.

31 Terah took his son Abram, his grandson Lot son of Haran, and his daughter-in-law Sarai, the wife of his son Abram, and together they set out from Ur of the Chaldeans to go to Canaan. But when they came to Harran, they settled there.

32 Terah lived 205 years, and he died in Harran.

The Call of Abram

12 The Homeboy had said to Abram, "Go from your country, your people and your father's household to the land I will show you.

> 2 "I will make you into a great nation,
>   and I will bless you;
> I will make your name great,
>   and you will be a blessing.
> 3 I will bless those who bless you,
>   and whoever curses you I will curse;
> and all peoples on earth
>   will be blessed through you."

4 So Abram went, as the Homeboy had told him; and Lot went with him. Abram was seventy-five years old when he set out from Harran. 5 He took his wife Sarai, his nephew Lot, all the possessions they had accumulated and the people they had acquired in Harran, and they set out for the land of Canaan, and they arrived there.

6 Abram traveled through the land as far as the site of the great tree of Moreh at Shechem. At that time the Canaanites were in the land. 7 The Homeboy appeared to Abram and said, "To your offspring I will give this land." So he built an altar there to the Homeboy, who had appeared to him.

8 From there he went on toward the hills east of Bethel and pitched his tent, with Bethel on the west and Ai on the east.

There he built an altar to the Homeboy and called on the name of the Homeboy.

9 Then Abram set out and continued toward the Negev.

Abram in Egypt

10 Now there was a famine in the land, and Abram went down to Egypt to live there for a while because the famine was severe. 11 As he was about to enter Egypt, he said to his wife Sarai, "I know what a beautiful woman you are. 12 When the Egyptians see you, they will say, 'This is his wife.' Then they will kill me but will let you live. 13 Say you are my sister, so that I will be treated well for your sake and my life will be spared because of you."

14 When Abram came to Egypt, the Egyptians saw that Sarai was a very beautiful woman. 15 And when Pharaoh's officials saw her, they praised her to Pharaoh, and she was taken into his palace. 16 He treated Abram well for her sake, and Abram acquired sheep and cattle, male and female donkeys, male and female servants, and camels.

17 But the Homeboy inflicted serious diseases on Pharaoh and his household because of Abram's wife Sarai. 18 So Pharaoh summoned Abram. "What have you done to me?" he said. "Why didn't you tell me she was your wife? 19 Why did you say, 'She is my sister,' so that I took her to be my wife? Now then, here is your wife. Take her and go!" 20 Then Pharaoh gave orders about Abram to his men, and they sent him on his way, with his wife and everything he had.

Abram and Lot Separate

13 So Abram went up from Egypt to the Negev, with his wife and everything he had, and Lot went with him. 2 Abram had become very wealthy in livestock and in silver and gold.

3 From the Negev he went from place to place until he came to Bethel, to the place between Bethel and Ai where his tent had been earlier 4 and where he had first built an altar. There Abram called on the name of the Holy Homeboy.

5 Now Lot, who was moving about with Abram, also had flocks and herds and tents. 6 But the land could not support them while they stayed together, for their possessions were so great that they were not able to stay together. 7 And quarreling arose between Abram's herders and Lot's. The Canaanites and Perizzites were also living in the land at that time.

8 So Abram said to Lot, "Let's not have any quarreling between you and me, or between your herders and mine, for we are close relatives. 9 Is not the whole land before you? Let's part company. If you go to the left, I'll go to the right; if you go to the right, I'll go to the left."

10 Lot looked around and saw that the whole plain of the Jordan toward Zoar was well watered, like the garden of the Homeboy, like the land of Egypt. (This was before the Homeboy destroyed Sodom and Gomorrah.) 11 So Lot chose for himself the whole plain of the Jordan and set out toward the east. The two men parted company: 12 Abram lived in the land of Canaan, while Lot lived among the cities of the plain and pitched his tents near Sodom. 13 Now the people of Sodom were wicked and were sinning greatly against the Homeboy.

14 The Homeboy said to Abram after Lot had parted from him, "Look around from where you are, to the north and south, to the east and west. 15 All the land that you see I will give to you and your offspring forever. 16 I will make your offspring like the dust of the earth, so that if anyone could count the dust, then your offspring could be counted. 17 Go, walk through the length and breadth of the land, for I am giving it to you."

18 So Abram went to live near the great trees of Mamre at Hebron, where he pitched his tents. There he built an altar to the Homeboy.

Abram Rescues Lot

14 At the time when Amraphel was king of Shinar, Arioch king of Ellasar, Kedorlaomer king of Elam and Tidal king of Goyim, 2 these kings went to war against Bera king of Sodom, Birsha king of Gomorrah, Shinab king of Admah, Shemeber king of Zeboyim, and the king of Bela (that is, Zoar).

3 All these latter kings joined forces in the Valley of Siddim (that is, the Dead Sea Valley). 4 For twelve years they had been subject to Kedorlaomer, but in the thirteenth year they rebelled.

5 In the fourteenth year, Kedorlaomer and the kings allied with him went out and defeated the Rephaites in Ashteroth Karnaim, the Zuzites in Ham, the Emites in Shaveh Kiriathaim 6 and the Horites in the hill country of Seir, as far as El Paran near the desert. 7 Then they turned back and went to En Mishpat (that is, Kadesh), and they conquered the whole territory of the Amalekites, as well as the Amorites who were living in Hazezon Tamar.

8 Then the king of Sodom, the king of Gomorrah, the king of Admah, the king of Zeboyim and the king of Bela (that is, Zoar) marched out and drew up their battle lines in the Valley of Siddim 9 against Kedorlaomer king of Elam, Tidal king of Goyim, Amraphel king of Shinar and Arioch king of Ellasar— four kings against five. 10 Now the Valley of Siddim was full of tar pits, and when the kings of Sodom and Gomorrah fled, some of the men fell into them and the rest fled to the hills. 11 The four kings seized all the goods of Sodom and Gomorrah and all their food; then they went away. 12 They also carried off Abram's nephew Lot and his possessions, since he was living in Sodom.

13 A man who had escaped came and reported this to Abram the Hebrew. Now Abram was living near the great trees of Mamre the Amorite, a brother of Eshkol and Aner, all of whom were allied with Abram. 14 When Abram heard that his relative had been taken captive, he called out the 318 trained men born in his household and went in pursuit as far as Dan. 15 During the night Abram divided his men to attack them and he routed them, pursuing them as far as Hobah, north of Damascus. 16 He recovered all the goods and brought back his relative Lot and his possessions, together with the women and the other people.

17 After Abram returned from defeating Kedorlaomer and the kings allied with him, the king of Sodom came out to meet him in the Valley of Shaveh (that is, the King's Valley).

18 Then Melchizedek king of Salem brought out bread and malt liquor. He was priest of The Big Gangster of the Most High,

19 and he blessed Abram, saying,
  "Blessed be Abram by The Big Gangster of the Most High,

Creator of heaven and earth.

20 And praise be to The Big Gangster of the Most High, who delivered your enemies into your hand."

Then Abram gave him a tenth of everything.

21 The king of Sodom said to Abram, "Give me the people and keep the goods for yourself."

22 But Abram said to the king of Sodom, "With raised hand I have sworn an oath to the Homeboy, The Big Gangster of the Most High, Creator of heaven and earth, 23 that I will accept nothing belonging to you, not even a thread or the strap of a sandal, so that you will never be able to say, 'I made Abram rich.' 24 I will accept nothing but what my men have eaten and the share that belongs to the men who went with me—to Aner, Eshkol and Mamre. Let them have their share."

The Homeboy's Covenant With Abram

15 After this, the word of the Homeboy came to Abram in a vision:

"Do not be afraid, Abram.
  I am your shield,
  your very great reward."

2 But Abram said, "Sovereign Homeboy, what can you give me since I remain childless and the one who will inherit my estate is Eliezer of Damascus?" 3 And Abram said, "You have given me no children; so a servant in my household will be my heir."

4 Then the word of the Homeboy came to him: "This man will not be your heir, but a son who is your own flesh and blood will be your heir." 5 He took him outside and said, "Look up at the sky and count the stars—if indeed you can count them." Then he said to him, "So shall your offspring be."

6 Abram believed the Homeboy, and he credited it to him as righteousness.

7 He also said to him, "I am the Homeboy, who brought you out of Ur of the Chaldeans to give you this land to take possession of it."

8 But Abram said, "Sovereign Gangster-in-the-Sky, how can I know that I will gain possession of it?"

9 So the Homeboy said to him, "Bring me a heifer, a goat and a ram, each three years old, along with a dove and a young pigeon."

10 Abram brought all these to him, cut them in two and arranged the halves opposite each other; the birds, however, he did not cut in half. 11 Then birds of prey came down on the carcasses, but Abram drove them away.

12 As the sun was setting, Abram fell into a deep sleep, and a thick and dreadful darkness came over him. 13 Then the Homeboy said to him, "Know for certain that for four hundred years your descendants will be strangers in a country not their own and that they will be enslaved and mistreated there. 14 But I will punish the nation they serve as slaves, and afterward they will come out with great possessions. 15 You, however, will go to your ancestors in peace and be buried at a good old age. 16 In the fourth generation your descendants will come back here, for the sin of the Amorites has not yet reached its full measure."

17 When the sun had set and darkness had fallen, a smoking firepot with a blazing torch appeared and passed between the pieces. 18 On that day the Homeboy made a covenant with Abram and said, "To your descendants I give this land, from the Wadi of Egypt to the great river, the Euphrates— 19 the land of the Kenites, Kenizzites, Kadmonites, 20 Hittites, Perizzites, Rephaites, 21 Amorites, Canaanites, Girgashites and Jebusites."

Hagar and Ishmael

16 Now Sarai, Abram's wife, had borne him no children. But she had an Egyptian slave named Hagar; 2 so she said to Abram, "The Homeboy has kept me from having children. Go, sleep with my slave; perhaps I can build a family through her."

Abram agreed to what Sarai said. 3 So after Abram had been living in Canaan ten years, Sarai his wife took her Egyptian slave Hagar and gave her to her husband to be his wife. 4 Abram slept with Hagar, and she got pregnant.

When Hagar knew she was pregnant, she began to look down upon Sarai. 5 Then Sarai said to Abram, "You are responsible for the wrong I am suffering. I put my slave in your arms, and now that she knows she is pregnant, she despises me. May the Homeboy judge between you and me."

6 "Your slave is in your hands," Abram said. "Do with her whatever you think best." Then Sarai mistreated Hagar; so she fled from her.

7 The angel of the Holy Homeboy found Hagar near a spring in the desert; it was the spring that is beside the road to Shur. 8 And he said, "Hagar, slave of Sarai, where have you come from, and where are you going?"

"I'm running away from my mistress Sarai," she answered.

9 Then the angel of the Homeboy told her, "Go back to your mistress and submit to her." 10 The angel added, "I will increase your descendants so much that they will be too numerous to count."

11 The angel of the Holy Homeboy also said to her:
"You are now pregnant
    and you will give birth to a son.
You shall name him Ishmael,
    for the Holy Homeboy has heard of your misery.
12 He will be a wild donkey of a man;
    his hand will be against everyone
    and everyone's hand against him,
and he will live in hostility
    toward all his brothers."

13 She gave this name to the Homeboy who spoke to her: "You are The Big Gangster who sees me," for she said, "I have now seen the One who sees me." 14 That is why the well was called Big Gangster Sees; it is still there, between Kadesh and Bered.

15 So Hagar bore Abram a son, and Abram gave the name Ishmael to the son she had borne. 16 Abram was eighty-six years old when Hagar bore him Ishmael.

The Covenant of Circumcision

17 When Abram was ninety-nine years old, the Homeboy appeared to him and said, "I am The Big Gangster Almighty; walk before me faithfully and be blameless. 2 Then I will make my covenant between me and you and will greatly increase your numbers."

3 Abram fell facedown, and The Big Gangster said to him, 4 "As for me, this is my covenant with you: You will be the father of many nations. 5 No longer will you be called Abram; your name will be Abraham, for I have made you a father of many nations. 6 I will make you very fruitful; I will make nations of you, and kings will come from you. 7 I will establish my covenant as an everlasting covenant between me and you and your descendants after you for the generations to come, to be your The Big Gangster and Big Gangster of your descendants after you. 8 The whole land of Canaan, where you now reside as a foreigner, I will give as an everlasting possession to you and your descendants after you; and I will be their The Big Gangster."

9 Then The Big Gangster said to Abraham, "As for you, you must keep my covenant, you and your descendants after you for the generations to come. 10 This is my covenant with you and your descendants after you, the covenant you are to keep: Every male among you shall be circumcised. 11 You are to undergo circumcision, and it will be the sign of the covenant between me and you. 12 For the generations to come every male among you who is eight days old must be circumcised, including those born in your household or bought with money from a foreigner—those who are not your offspring. 13 Whether born in your household they must be circumcised. My covenant in your flesh is to be an everlasting covenant. 14 Any uncircumcised male, who has not been circumcised in the flesh, will be cut off from his people; he has broken my covenant."

15 The Big Gangster also said to Abraham, "As for Sarai your wife, you are no longer to call her Sarai; her name will be

Sarah. 16 I will bless her and will surely give you a son by her. I will bless her so that she will be the mother of nations; kings of peoples will come from her."

17 Abraham fell facedown; he laughed and said to himself, "Will a son be born to a man a hundred years old? Will Sarah bear a child at the age of ninety?" 18 And Abraham said to The Big Gangster, "If only Ishmael might live under your blessing!"

19 Then The Big Gangster said, "Yes, but your wife Sarah will bear you a son, and you will call him Isaac. I will establish my covenant with him as an everlasting covenant for his descendants after him. 20 And as for Ishmael, I have heard you: I will surely bless him; I will make him fruitful and will greatly increase his numbers. He will be the father of twelve rulers, and I will make him into a great nation. 21 But my covenant I will establish with Isaac, whom Sarah will bear to you by this time next year." 22 When he had finished speaking with Abraham, The Big Gangster went up from him.

23 On that very day Abraham took his son Ishmael and all those born in his household, every male in his household, and circumcised them, as The Big Gangster told him. 24 Abraham was ninety-nine years old when he was circumcised, 25 and his son Ishmael was thirteen; 26 Abraham and his son Ishmael were both circumcised on that very day. 27 And every male in Abraham's household, including those born in his household or bought from a foreigner, was circumcised with him.

The Three Visitors

18 The Homeboy appeared to Abraham near the great trees of Mamre while he was sitting at the entrance to his tent in the heat of the day. 2 Abraham looked up and saw three men standing nearby. When he saw them, he hurried from the entrance of his tent to meet them and bowed low to the ground.

3 He said, "If I have found favor in your eyes, my homies, do not pass your servant by. 4 Let a little water be brought, and then you may all wash your feet and rest under this tree. 5 Let me get you something to eat, so you can be refreshed and then go on your way—now that you have come to your servant."

"Very well," they answered, "do as you say."

6 So Abraham hurried into the tent to Sarah. "Quick," he said, "make some food for the homies who are visiting us."

7 Then he ran to the herd and selected a choice, tender calf and gave it to a servant, who hurried to prepare it. 8 He then brought some curds and milk and the calf that had been prepared, and set these before them. While they ate, he stood near them under a tree.

9 "Where is your wife Sarah?" they asked him.

"There, in the tent," he said.

10 Then one of them said, "I will surely return to you about this time next year, and Sarah your wife will have a son."

Now Sarah was listening at the entrance to the tent, which was behind him. 11 Abraham and Sarah were already very old, and Sarah was past the age of childbearing. 12 So Sarah laughed to herself as she thought, "After I am worn out and my husband is old, will I now have this pleasure?"

13 Then the Holy Homeboy said to Abraham, "Why did Sarah laugh and say, 'Will I really have a child, now that I am old?' 14 Is anything too hard for the Homeboy? I will return to you at the appointed time next year, and Sarah will have a son."

15 Sarah was afraid, so she lied and said, "I did not laugh."

But he said, "Yes, you did laugh."

Abraham Pleads for Sodom

16 When the men got up to leave, they looked down toward Sodom, and Abraham walked along with them to see them on their way. 17 Then the Homeboy said, "Shall I hide from Abraham what I am about to do? 18 Abraham will surely become a great and powerful nation, and all nations on earth will be blessed through him. 19 For I have chosen him, so that he will direct his children and his household after him to keep the way of the Homeboy by doing what is right and just, so that the Homeboy will bring about for Abraham what he has promised him."

20 Then the Homeboy said, "The outcry against Sodom and Gomorrah is so great and their sin so grievous 21 that I will go down and see if what they have done is as bad as the outcry that has reached me. If not, I will know."

22 The men turned away and went toward Sodom, but Abraham remained standing before the Homeboy. 23 Then Abraham approached him and said: "Will you sweep away the righteous with the wicked? 24 What if there are fifty righteous people in the city? Will you really sweep it away and not spare the place for the sake of the fifty righteous people in it? 25 Far be it from you to do such a thing—to kill the righteous with the wicked, treating the righteous and the wicked alike. Far be it from you! Will not the Judge of all the earth do right?" Abraham sought to bargain with the Holy Homeboy.

26 The Homeboy said, "If I find fifty righteous people in the city of Sodom, I will spare the whole place for their sake."

27 Then Abraham spoke up again: "Now that I have been so bold as to speak to the Homeboy, though I am nothing but dust and ashes, 28 what if the number of the righteous is five less than fifty? Will you destroy the whole city for lack of five people?"

"If I find forty-five there," he said, "I will not destroy it."

29 Once again he spoke to him, "What if only forty are found there?"

He said, "For the sake of forty, I will not do it."

30 Then he said, "May the Homeboy not be angry, but let me speak. What if only thirty can be found there?"

He answered, "I will not do it if I find thirty there."

31 Abraham said, "Now that I have been so bold as to speak to the Homeboy, what if only twenty can be found there?"

He said, "For the sake of twenty, I will not destroy it."

32 Then he said, "May the Homeboy not be angry, but let me speak just once more. What if only ten can be found there?"

He answered, "For the sake of ten, I will not destroy it."

33 When the Homeboy had finished speaking with Abraham, he left, and Abraham returned home.

Sodom and Gomorrah Destroyed

19 The two angels arrived at Sodom in the evening, and Lot was sitting in the gateway of the city. When he saw them, he got up to meet them and bowed down with his face to the ground. 2 "My homies," he said, "please turn aside to your

servant's house. You can wash your feet and spend the night and then go on your way early in the morning."

"No," they answered, "we will spend the night in the square."

3 But he insisted so strongly that they did go with him and entered his house. He prepared a meal for them, baking bread without yeast, and they ate. 4 Before they had gone to bed, all the men from every part of the city of Sodom—both young and old—surrounded the house. 5 They called to Lot, "Where are the men who came to you tonight? Bring them out to us so that we can bust their booties."

6 Lot went outside to meet them and shut the door behind him 7 and said, "No, my friends. Don't do this wicked thing. 8 Look, I have two daughters who have never slept with a man. Let me bring them out to you, and you can do what you like with them. But don't do anything to these men, for they have come under the protection of my roof."

9 "Get out of our way," they replied. "This fellow came here as a foreigner, and now he wants to play the judge! We'll treat you worse than them." They kept bringing pressure on Lot and moved forward to break down the door.

10 But the men inside reached out and pulled Lot back into the house and shut the door. 11 Then they struck the men who were at the door of the house, young and old, with blindness so that they could not find the door.

12 The two men said to Lot, "Do you have anyone else here—sons-in-law, sons or daughters, or anyone else in the city who belongs to you? Get them out of here, 13 because we are going to destroy this place. The outcry to the Homeboy against its people is so great that he has sent us to destroy it."

14 So Lot went out and spoke to his sons-in-law, who were pledged to marry his daughters. He said, "Hurry and get out of this place, because the Homeboy is about to destroy the city!" But his sons-in-law thought he was joking.

15 With the coming of dawn, the angels urged Lot, saying, "Hurry! Take your wife and your two daughters who are here, or you will be swept away when the city is punished."

16 When he hesitated, the men grasped his hand and the hands of his wife and of his two daughters and led them safely

out of the city, for the Holy Homeboy was merciful to them. 17 As soon as they had brought them out, one of them said, "Flee for your lives! Don't look back, and don't stop anywhere in the plain! Flee to the mountains or you will be swept away!"

18 But Lot said to them, "No, my homies, please! 19 Your servant has found favor in your eyes, and you have shown great kindness to me in sparing my life. But I can't flee to the mountains; this disaster will overtake me, and I'll die. 20 Look, here is a town near enough to run to, and it is small. Let me flee to it—it is very small, isn't it? Then my life will be spared."

21 He said to him, "Very well, I will grant this request too; I will not overthrow the town you speak of. 22 But flee there quickly, because I cannot do anything until you reach it." (That is why the town was called Zoar.)

23 By the time Lot reached Zoar, the sun had risen over the land. 24 Then the Homeboy rained down burning sulfur on Sodom and Gomorrah—from the Holy Homeboy out of the heavens. 25 Thus he overthrew those cities and the entire plain, destroying all those living in the cities—and also the vegetation in the land. 26 But Lot's wife looked back, and she became a pillar of salt.

27 Early the next morning Abraham got up and returned to the place where he had stood before the Homeboy. 28 He looked down toward Sodom and Gomorrah, toward all the land of the plain, and he saw dense smoke rising from the land, like smoke from a furnace.

29 So when The Big Gangster destroyed the cities of the plain, he remembered Abraham, and he brought Lot out of the catastrophe that overthrew the cities where Lot had lived.

Lot and His Daughters

30 Lot and his two daughters left Zoar and settled in the mountains, for he was afraid to stay in Zoar. He and his two daughters lived in a cave. 31 One day the older daughter said to the younger, "Our father is old, and there is no man around here to give us children—as is the custom all over the earth. 32 Let's get our father to drink malt liquor and then sleep with him and preserve our family line through our father."

33 That night they got their father to drink malt liquor, and the older daughter went in and slept with him. He was not aware of it when she lay down or when she got up.

34 The next day the older daughter said to the younger, "Last night I slept with my father. Let's get him to drink malt liquor again tonight, and you go in and sleep with him so we can preserve our family line through our father." 35 So they got their father to drink malt liquor that night also, and the younger daughter went in and slept with him. Again he was not aware of it when she lay down or when she got up.

36 So both of Lot's daughters became pregnant by their father. 37 The older daughter had a son, and she named him Moab; he is the father of the Moabites of today. 38 The younger daughter also had a son, and she named him Ben-Ammi; he is the father of the Ammonites of today.

Abraham and Abimelek

20 Now Abraham moved on from there into the region of the Negev and lived between Kadesh and Shur. For a while he stayed in Gerar, 2 and there Abraham said of his wife Sarah, "She is my sister." Then Abimelek king of Gerar sent for Sarah and took her.

3 But The Big Gangster came to Abimelek in a dream one night and said to him, "You are as good as dead because of the woman you have taken; she is a married woman."

4 Now Abimelek had not gone near her, so he said, "Homeboy, will you destroy an innocent nation? 5 Did he not say to me, 'She is my sister,' and didn't she also say, 'He is my brother'? I have done this with a clear conscience and clean hands."

6 Then The Big Gangster said to him in the dream, "Yes, I know you did this with a clear conscience, and so I have kept you from sinning against me. That is why I did not let you touch her. 7 Now return the man's wife, for he is a prophet, and he will pray for you and you will live. But if you do not return her, you may be sure that you and all who belong to you will die."

8 Early the next morning Abimelek summoned all his officials, and when he told them all that had happened, they were very much afraid. 9 Then Abimelek called Abraham in and said,

"What have you done to us? How have I wronged you that you have brought such great guilt upon me and my kingdom? You have done things to me that should never be done." 10 And Abimelek asked Abraham, "What was your reason for doing this?"

11 Abraham replied, "I said to myself, 'There is surely no fear of The Big Gangster in this place, and they will kill me because of my wife.' 12 Besides, she really is my sister, the daughter of my father though not of my mother; and she became my wife. 13 And when The Big Gangster had me wander from my father's household, I said to her, 'This is how you can show your love to me: Everywhere we go, say of me, "He is my brother."'"

14 Then Abimelek brought sheep and cattle and male and female slaves and gave them to Abraham, and he returned Sarah his wife to him. 15 And Abimelek said, "My land is before you; live wherever you like."

16 To Sarah he said, "I am giving your brother a thousand shekels of silver. This is to cover the offense against you before all who are with you; you are completely vindicated."

17 Then Abraham prayed to The Big Gangster, and The Big Gangster healed Abimelek, his wife and his female slaves so they could have children again, 18 for the Homeboy had kept all the women in Abimelek's household from conceiving because of Abraham's wife Sarah.

The Birth of Isaac

21 Now the Homeboy was gracious to Sarah as he had said, and the Homeboy did for Sarah what he had promised. 2 Sarah became pregnant and bore a son to Abraham in his old age, at the very time The Big Gangster had promised him. 3 Abraham gave the name Isaac to the son Sarah bore him. 4 When his son Isaac was eight days old, Abraham circumcised him, as The Big Gangster commanded him. 5 Abraham was a hundred years old when his son Isaac was born to him.

6 Sarah said, "The Big Gangster has brought me laughter, and everyone who hears about this will laugh with me." 7 And she added, "Who would have said to Abraham that Sarah would nurse children? Yet I have borne him a son in his old age."

Hagar and Ishmael Sent Away

8 The child grew and was weaned, and on the day Isaac was weaned Abraham held a great feast. 9 But Sarah saw that the son whom Hagar the Egyptian had borne to Abraham was mocking and screwing around, 10 and she said to Abraham, "Get rid of that slave woman and her son, for that woman's son will never share in the inheritance with my son Isaac."

11 The matter distressed Abraham greatly because it concerned his son. 12 But The Big Gangster said to him, "Do not be so distressed about the boy and your slave woman. Listen to whatever Sarah tells you, because it is through Isaac that your offspring will be determined. 13 I will make the son of the slave into a nation also, because he is your offspring."

14 Early the next morning Abraham took some food and a skin of water and gave them to Hagar. He set them on her shoulders and then sent her off with the boy. She went on her way and wandered in the Desert of Beersheba.

15 When the water in the skin was gone, she put the boy under one of the bushes. 16 Then she went off and sat down about a stone's throw away, for she thought, "I cannot watch the boy die." And as she sat there, she began to sob.

17 The Big Gangster heard the boy crying, and the angel of The Big Gangster called to Hagar from heaven and said to her, "What is the matter, Hagar? Do not be afraid; The Big Gangster has heard the boy crying as he lies there. 18 Lift the boy up and take him by the hand, for I will make him into a great nation."

19 Then The Big Gangster opened her eyes and she saw a well of water. So she went and filled the skin with water and gave the boy a drink.

20 The Big Gangster was with the boy as he grew up. He lived in the desert and became an archer. 21 While he was living in the Desert of Paran, his mother got a wife for him from Egypt.

The Treaty at Beersheba

22 At that time Abimelek and Phicol the commander of his forces said to Abraham, "The Big Gangster is with you in everything you do. 23 Now swear to me here before The Big Gangster

that you will not deal falsely with me or my children or my descendants. Show to me and the country where you now reside as a foreigner the same kindness I have shown to you."

24 Abraham said, "I swear it."

25 Then Abraham complained to Abimelek about a well of water that Abimelek's servants had seized. 26 But Abimelek said, "I don't know who has done this. You did not tell me, and I heard about it only today."

27 So Abraham brought sheep and cattle and gave them to Abimelek, and the two men made a treaty. 28 Abraham set apart seven ewe lambs from the flock, 29 and Abimelek asked Abraham, "What is the meaning of these seven ewe lambs you have set apart by themselves?"

30 He replied, "Accept these seven lambs from my hand as a witness that I dug this well."

31 So that place was called Beersheba, because the two men swore an oath there.

32 After the treaty had been made at Beersheba, Abimelek and Phicol the commander of his forces returned to the land of the Philistines. 33 Abraham planted a tamarisk tree in Beersheba, and there he called on the name of the Holy Homeboy, the Eternal The Big Gangster. 34 And Abraham stayed in the land of the Philistines for a long time.

Abraham Tested

22 Sometime later The Big Gangster tested Abraham. He said to him, "Abraham!"

"Here I am," he replied.

2 Then The Big Gangster said, "Take your son, whom you love—Isaac—and go to the region of Moriah. Sacrifice him there as a burnt offering on a mountain I will show you."

3 Early the next morning Abraham got up and loaded his donkey. He took with him two of his servants and his son Isaac. When he had cut enough wood for the burnt offering, he set out for the place The Big Gangster had told him about. 4 On the third day Abraham looked up and saw the place in the distance. 5 He said to his servants, "Stay here with the donkey while I and

the boy go over there. We will worship and then we will come back to you."

6 Abraham took the wood for the burnt offering and placed it on his son Isaac, and he himself carried the fire and the knife. As the two of them went on together, 7 Isaac spoke up and said to his father Abraham, "Father?"

"Yes, my son?" Abraham replied.

"The fire and wood are here," Isaac said, "but where is the lamb for the burnt offering?"

8 Abraham answered, "The Big Gangster himself will provide the lamb for the burnt offering, my son." And the two of them went on together.

9 When they reached the place The Big Gangster had told him about, Abraham built an altar there and arranged the wood on it. He bound his son Isaac and laid him on the altar, on top of the wood. 10 Then he reached out his hand and took the knife to slaughter his son. 11 But the angel of the Homeboy called out to him from heaven, "Abraham! Abraham!"

"Here I am," he replied.

12 "Do not lay a hand on the boy," he said. "Do not do anything to him. Now I know that you fear The Big Gangster, because you have not withheld from me your son."

13 Abraham looked up and there in a thicket he saw a ram caught by its horns. He went over and took the ram and sacrificed it as a burnt offering instead of his son. 14 So Abraham called that place The Holy Homeboy Will Provide. And to this day it is said, "On the mountain of the Homeboy it will be provided."

15 The angel of the Homeboy called to Abraham from heaven a second time 16 and said, "I swear by myself, declares the Homeboy, that because you have done this and have not withheld your son, your only son, 17 I will surely bless you and make your descendants as numerous as the stars in the sky and as the sand on the seashore. Your descendants will take possession of the cities of their enemies, 18 and through your offspring all nations on earth will be blessed, because you have obeyed me."

19 Then Abraham returned to his servants, and they set off together for Beersheba. And Abraham stayed in Beersheba.

Nahor's Sons

20 Sometime later Abraham was told, "Milkah is also a mother; she has borne sons to your brother Nahor: 21 Uz the firstborn, Buz his brother, Kemuel (the father of Aram), 22 Kesed, Hazo, Pildash, Jidlaph and Bethuel." 23 Bethuel became the father of Rebekah. Milkah bore these eight sons to Abraham's brother Nahor. 24 His concubine, whose name was Reumah, also had sons: Tebah, Gaham, Tahash and Maakah.

The Death of Sarah

23 Sarah lived to be a hundred and twenty-seven years old. 2 She died at Kiriath Arba (that is, Hebron) in the land of Canaan, and Abraham went to mourn for Sarah and to weep over her.

3 Then Abraham rose from beside his dead wife and spoke to the Hittites. He said, 4 "I am a foreigner and stranger among you. Sell me some property for a burial site here so I can bury my dead."

5 The Hittites replied to Abraham, 6 "Sir, listen to us. You are a mighty prince among us. Bury your dead in the choicest of our tombs. None of us will refuse you his tomb for burying your dead."

7 Then Abraham rose and bowed down before the people of the land, the Hittites. 8 He said to them, "If you are willing to let me bury my dead, then listen to me and intercede with Ephron son of Zohar on my behalf 9 so he will sell me the cave of Machpelah, which belongs to him and is at the end of his field. Ask him to sell it to me for the full price as a burial site among you."

10 Ephron the Hittite was sitting among his people and he replied to Abraham in the hearing of all the Hittites who had come to the gate of his city. 11 "No," he said. "Listen to me; I give you the field, and I give you the cave that is in it. I give it to you in the presence of my people. Bury your dead."

12 Again Abraham bowed down before the people of the land 13 and he said to Ephron in their hearing, "Listen to me, if

you will. I will pay the price of the field. Accept it from me so I can bury my dead there."

14 Ephron answered Abraham, 15 "Listen to me, my homie; the land is worth four hundred shekels of silver, but what is that between you and me? Bury your dead."

16 Abraham agreed to Ephron's terms and weighed out for him the price he had named in the hearing of the Hittites: four hundred shekels of silver, according to the weight current among the merchants.

17 So Ephron's field in Machpelah near Mamre—both the field and the cave in it, and all the trees within the borders of the field—was deeded 18 to Abraham as his property in the presence of all the Hittites who had come to the gate of the city. 19 Afterward Abraham buried his wife Sarah in the cave in the field of Machpelah near Mamre (which is at Hebron) in the land of Canaan. 20 So the field and the cave in it were deeded to Abraham by the Hittites as a burial site.

Isaac and Rebekah

24 Abraham was now very old, and the Holy Homeboy had blessed him in every way. 2 He said to the senior servant in his household, the one in charge of all that he had, "Put your hand under my thigh. 3 I want you to swear by the Holy Homeboy, The Big Gangster of heaven and The Big Gangster of earth, that you will not get a wife for my son from the daughters of the Canaanites, among whom I am living, 4 but will go to my country and my own relatives and get a wife for my son Isaac."

5 The servant asked him, "What if the woman is unwilling to come back with me to this land? Shall I then take your son back to the country you came from?"

6 "Make sure that you do not take my son back there," Abraham said. 7 "The Homeboy, The Big Gangster of heaven, who brought me out of my father's household and my native land and who spoke to me and promised me on oath, saying, 'To your offspring I will give this land'—he will send his angel before you so that you can get a wife for my son from there. 8 If the woman is unwilling to come back with you, then you will be released from this oath of mine. Only do not take my son back

there." 9 So the servant put his hand under the thigh of his master Abraham and swore an oath to him concerning this matter.

10 Then the servant left, taking with him ten of his master's camels loaded with all kinds of good things from his master. He set out for Aram Naharaim and made his way to the town of Nahor. 11 He had the camels kneel down near the well outside the town; it was toward evening, the time the women go out to draw water.

12 Then he prayed, "Homeboy, The Big Gangster of my master Abraham, make me successful today, and show kindness to my master Abraham. 13 See, I am standing beside this spring, and the daughters of the townspeople are coming out to draw water. 14 May it be that when I say to a young woman, 'Please let down your jar that I may have a drink,' and she says, 'Drink, and I'll water your camels too'—let her be the one you have chosen for your servant Isaac. By this I will know that you have shown kindness to my master."

15 Before he had finished praying, Rebekah came out with her jar on her shoulder. She was the daughter of Bethuel son of Milkah, who was the wife of Abraham's brother Nahor. 16 The woman was very beautiful, a virgin; no man had ever slept with her. She went down to the spring, filled her jar and came up again.

17 The servant hurried to meet her and said, "Please give me a little water from your jar."

18 "Drink, my tired homie," she said, and quickly lowered the jar to her hands and gave him a drink.

19 After she had given him a drink, she said, "I'll draw water for your camels too, until they have had enough to drink." 20 So she quickly emptied her jar into the trough, ran back to the well to draw more water, and drew enough for all his camels. 21 Without saying a word, the man watched her closely to learn whether or not the Holy Homeboy had made his journey successful.

22 When the camels had finished drinking, the man took out a gold nose ring and two gold bracelets weighing ten shekels. 23 Then he asked, "Whose daughter are you? Please tell me, is there room in your father's house for us to spend the night?"

24 She answered him, "I am the daughter of Bethuel, the son that Milkah bore to Nahor." 25 And she added, "We have plenty of straw and fodder, as well as room for you to spend the night."

26 Then the man bowed down and worshiped the Holy Homeboy, 27 saying, "Praise be to the Homeboy, The Big Gangster of my master Abraham, who has not abandoned his kindness and faithfulness to my master. As for me, the Homeboy has led me on the journey to the house of my master's relatives."

28 The young woman ran and told her mother's household about these things. 29 Now Rebekah had a brother named Laban, and he hurried out to the man at the spring. 30 As soon as he had seen the nose ring, and the bracelets on his sister's arms, and had heard Rebekah tell what the man said to her, he went out to the man and found him standing by the camels near the spring. 31 "Come, you who are blessed by the Holy Homeboy," he said. "Why are you standing out here? I have prepared the house and a place for the camels."

32 So the man went to the house, and the camels were unloaded. Straw and fodder were brought for the camels, and water for him and his men to wash their feet. 33 Then food was set before him, but he said, "I will not eat until I have told you what I have to say."

"Then tell us," Laban said.

34 So he said, "I am Abraham's servant. 35 The Homeboy has blessed my master abundantly, and he has become wealthy. He has given him sheep and cattle, silver and gold, male and female servants, and camels and donkeys. 36 My master's wife Sarah has borne him a son in her old age, and he has given him everything he owns. 37 And my master made me swear an oath, and said, 'You must not get a wife for my son from the daughters of the Canaanites, in whose land I live, 38 but go to my father's family and to my own clan, and get a wife for my son.'

39 "Then I asked my master, 'What if the woman will not come back with me?'

40 "He replied, 'The Homeboy, before whom I have walked faithfully, will send his angel with you and make your journey a success, so that you can get a wife for my son from my own clan and from my father's family. 41 You will be released from

my oath if, when you go to my clan, they refuse to give her to you—then you will be released from my oath.'

42 "When I came to the spring today, I said, 'Homeboy, The Big Gangster of my master Abraham, if you will, please grant success to the journey on which I have come. 43 See, I am standing beside this spring. If a young woman comes out to draw water and I say to her, "Please let me drink a little water from your jar," 44 and if she says to me, "Drink, and I'll draw water for your camels too," let her be the one the Homeboy has chosen for my master's son.'

45 "Before I finished praying in my heart, Rebekah came out, with her jar on her shoulder. She went down to the spring and drew water, and I said to her, 'Please give me a drink.'

46 "She quickly lowered her jar from her shoulder and said, 'Drink, and I'll water your camels too.' So I drank, and she watered the camels also.

47 "I asked her, 'Whose daughter are you?'

"She said, 'The daughter of Bethuel son of Nahor, whom Milkah bore to him.'

"Then I put the ring in her nose and the bracelets on her arms, 48 and I bowed down and worshiped the Holy Homeboy. I praised the Homeboy, The Big Gangster of my master Abraham, who had led me on the right road to get the granddaughter of my master's brother for his son. 49 Now if you will show kindness and faithfulness to my master, tell me; and if not, tell me, so I may know which way to turn."

50 Laban and Bethuel answered, "This is from the Homeboy-in-the-Sky; we can say nothing to you one way or the other. 51 Here is Rebekah; take her and go, and let her become the wife of your master's son, as the Homeboy has directed."

52 When Abraham's servant heard what they said, he bowed down to the ground before the Homeboy. 53 Then the servant brought out gold and silver jewelry and articles of clothing and gave them to Rebekah; he also gave costly gifts to her brother and to her mother. 54 Then he and the men who were with him ate and drank and spent the night there.

When they got up the next morning, he said, "Send me on my way to my master."

55 But her brother and her mother replied, "Let the young woman remain with us ten days or so; then you may go."

56 But he said to them, "Do not detain me, now that the Homeboy has granted success to my journey. Send me on my way so I may go to my master."

57 Then they said, "Let's call the young woman and ask her about it." 58 So they called Rebekah and asked her, "Will you go with this man?"

"I will go," she said.

59 So they sent their sister Rebekah on her way, along with her nurse and Abraham's servant and his men. 60 And they blessed Rebekah and said to her,

"Our sister, may you increase
   to thousands upon thousands;
may your offspring possess
   the cities of their enemies."

61 Then Rebekah and her attendants got ready and mounted the camels and went back with the man. So the servant took Rebekah and left.

62 Now Isaac had come from The Big Gangster Sees, for he was living in the Negev. 63 He went out to the field one evening to meditate, and as he looked up, he saw camels approaching. 64 Rebekah also looked up and saw Isaac. She got down from her camel 65 and asked the servant, "Who is that man in the field coming to meet us?"

"He is my master," the servant answered. So she took her veil and covered herself.

66 Then the servant told Isaac all he had done. 67 Isaac brought her into the tent of his mother Sarah, and he married Rebekah. So she became his wife, and he loved her; and Isaac was comforted after his mother's death.

The Death of Abraham

25 Abraham had taken another wife, whose name was Keturah. 2 She bore him Zimran, Jokshan, Medan, Midian, Ishbak and Shuah. 3 Jokshan was the father of Sheba

and Dedan; the descendants of Dedan were the Ashurites, the Letushites and the Leummites. 4 The sons of Midian were Ephah, Epher, Hanok, Abida and Eldaah. All these were descendants of Keturah.

5 Abraham left everything he owned to Isaac. 6 But while he was still living, he gave gifts to the sons of his concubines and sent them away from his son Isaac to the land of the east.

7 Abraham lived a hundred and seventy-five years. 8 Then Abraham breathed his last and died at a good old age, an old man and full of years; and he was gathered to his people. 9 His sons Isaac and Ishmael buried him in the cave of Machpelah near Mamre, in the field of Ephron son of Zohar the Hittite, 10 the field Abraham had bought from the Hittites. There Abraham was buried with his wife Sarah. 11 After Abraham's death, The Big Gangster blessed his son Isaac, who then lived near The Big Gangster Sees.

Ishmael's Sons

12 This is the account of the family line of Abraham's son Ishmael, whom Sarah's slave, Hagar the Egyptian, bore to Abraham.

13 These are the names of the sons of Ishmael, listed in the order of their birth: Nebaioth the firstborn of Ishmael, Kedar, Adbeel, Mibsam, 14 Mishma, Dumah, Massa, 15 Hadad, Tema, Jetur, Naphish and Kedemah. 16 These were the sons of Ishmael, and these are the names of the twelve tribal rulers according to their settlements and camps. 17 Ishmael lived a hundred and thirty-seven years. He breathed his last and died, and he was gathered to his people. 18 His descendants settled in the area from Havilah to Shur, near the eastern border of Egypt, as you go toward Ashur. And they lived in hostility toward all the tribes related to them.

Jacob and Esau

19 This is the account of the family line of Abraham's son Isaac.

Abraham became the father of Isaac, 20 and Isaac was forty years old when he married Rebekah daughter of Bethuel the Aramean from Paddan Aram and sister of Laban the Aramean.

21 Isaac prayed to the Homeboy on behalf of his wife, because she was childless. The Homeboy answered his prayer, and his wife Rebekah became pregnant. 22 The babies jostled each other within her, and she said, "Why is this happening to me?" So she went to inquire of the Homeboy.

23 The Homeboy said to her,
"Two nations are in your womb,
  and two peoples from within you will be separated;
one people will be stronger than the other,
  and the older will serve the younger."

24 When the time came for her to give birth, there were twin boys in her womb. 25 The first to come out was red, and his whole body was like a hairy garment; so they named him Esau. 26 After this, his brother came out, with his hand grasping Esau's heel; so he was named Jacob. Isaac was sixty years old when Rebekah gave birth to them.

27 The boys grew up, and Esau became a skillful hunter, a man of the open country, while Jacob was content to stay at home among the tents. 28 Isaac, who had a taste for wild game, loved Esau, but Rebekah loved Jacob.

29 Once when Jacob was cooking some stew, Esau came in from the open country, famished. 30 He said to Jacob, "Quick, let me have some of that red stew! I'm famished!" (That is why he was also called Edom.)

31 Jacob replied, "First sell me your birthright."

32 "Look, I am about to die," Esau said. "What good is the birthright to me?"

33 But Jacob said, "Swear to me first." So he swore an oath to him, selling his birthright to Jacob.

34 Then Jacob gave Esau some bread and some lentil stew. He ate and drank, and then got up and left.

So Esau despised his birthright.

Isaac and Abimelek

26 Now there was a famine in the land—besides the previous famine in Abraham's time—and Isaac went to Abimelek king of the Philistines in Gerar. 2 The Homeboy appeared to Isaac and said, "Do not go down to Egypt; live in the land where I tell you to live. 3 Stay in this land for a while, and I will be with you and will bless you. For to you and your descendants I will give all these lands and will confirm the oath I swore to your father Abraham. 4 I will make your descendants as numerous as the stars in the sky and will give them all these lands, and through your offspring all nations on earth will be blessed, 5 because Abraham obeyed me and did everything I required of him, keeping my commands, my decrees and my instructions." 6 So Isaac stayed in Gerar.

7 When the men of that place asked him about his wife, he said, "She is my sister," because he was afraid to say, "She is my wife." He thought, "The men of this place might kill me on account of Rebekah, because she is beautiful."

8 When Isaac had been there a long time, Abimelek king of the Philistines looked down from a window and saw Isaac caressing his wife Rebekah. 9 So Abimelek summoned Isaac and said, "She is really your wife! Why did you say, 'She is my sister'?"

Isaac answered him, "Because I thought I might lose my life on account of her."

10 Then Abimelek said, "What is this you have done to us? One of the men might well have slept with your wife, and you would have brought sin upon us."

11 So Abimelek gave orders to all the people: "Anyone who harms this man or his wife shall surely be put to death."

12 Isaac planted crops in that land and the same year reaped a hundredfold, because the Homeboy blessed him. 13 The man became rich, and his wealth continued to grow until he became very wealthy. 14 He had so many flocks and herds and servants that the Philistines envied him. 15 So all the wells that his father's servants had dug in the time of his father Abraham, the Philistines stopped up, filling them with earth.

16 Then Abimelek said to Isaac, "Move away from us; you have become too powerful for us."

17 So Isaac moved away from there and encamped in the Valley of Gerar, where he settled. 18 Isaac reopened the wells that had been dug in the time of his father Abraham, which the Philistines had stopped up after Abraham died, and he gave them the same names his father had given them.

19 Isaac's servants dug in the valley and discovered a well of fresh water there. 20 But the herders of Gerar quarreled with those of Isaac and said, "The water is ours!" So he named the well Esek, because they disputed with him. 21 Then they dug another well, but they quarreled over that one also; so he named it Sitnah. 22 He moved on from there and dug another well, and no one quarreled over it. He named it Rehoboth, saying, "Now the Homeboy has given us room and we will flourish in the land."

23 From there he went up to Beersheba. 24 That night the Homeboy appeared to him and said, "I am The Big Gangster of your father Abraham. Do not be afraid, for I am with you; I will bless you and will increase the number of your descendants for the sake of my servant Abraham."

25 Isaac built an altar there and called on the name of the Homeboy. There he pitched his tent, and there his servants dug a well.

26 Meanwhile, Abimelek had come to him from Gerar, with Ahuzzath his personal adviser and Phicol the commander of his forces. 27 Isaac asked them, "Why have you come to me, since you were hostile to me and sent me away?"

28 They answered, "We saw clearly that the Homeboy was with you; so we said, 'There ought to be a sworn agreement between us'—between us and you. Let us make a treaty with you 29 that you will do us no harm, just as we did not harm you but always treated you well and sent you away peacefully. And now you are blessed by the Homeboy."

30 Isaac then made a feast for them, and they ate and drank. 31 Early the next morning the men swore an oath to each other. Then Isaac sent them on their way, and they went away peacefully.

32 That day Isaac's servants came and told him about the well they had dug. They said, "We've found water!" 33 He called it Shibah, and to this day the name of the town has been Beersheba.

Jacob Takes Esau's Blessing

34 When Esau was forty years old, he married Judith daughter of Beeri the Hittite, and also Basemath daughter of Elon the Hittite. 35 They were a source of grief to Isaac and Rebekah.

27 When Isaac was old and his eyes were so weak that he could no longer see, he called for Esau his older son and said to him, "My son."

"Here I am," he answered.

2 Isaac said, "I am now an old man and don't know the day of my death. 3 Now then, get your equipment—your quiver and bow—and go out to the open country to hunt some wild game for me. 4 Prepare me the kind of tasty food I like and bring it to me to eat, so that I may give you my blessing before I die."

5 Now Rebekah was listening as Isaac spoke to his son Esau. When Esau left for the open country to hunt game and bring it back, 6 Rebekah said to her son Jacob, "Look, I overheard your father say to your brother Esau, 7 'Bring me some game and prepare me some tasty food to eat, so that I may give you my blessing in the presence of the Homeboy before I die.' 8 Now, my son, listen carefully and do what I tell you: 9 Go out to the flock and bring me two choice young goats, so I can prepare some tasty food for your father, just the way he likes it. 10 Then take it to your father to eat, so that he may give you his blessing before he dies."

11 Jacob said to Rebekah his mother, "But my brother Esau is a hairy man while I have smooth skin. 12 What if my father touches me? I would appear to be tricking him and would bring down a curse on myself rather than a blessing."

13 His mother said to him, "My son, let the curse fall on me. Just do what I say; go and get them for me."

14 So he went and got them and brought them to his mother, and she prepared some tasty food, just the way his father liked it. 15 Then Rebekah took the best clothes of Esau her older son,

which she had in the house, and put them on her younger son Jacob. 16 She also covered his hands and the smooth part of his neck with the goatskins. 17 Then she handed to her son Jacob the tasty food and the bread she had made.

18 He went to his father and said, "My father."

"Yes, my son," he answered. "Who is it?"

19 Jacob said to his father, "I am Esau your firstborn. I have done as you told me. Please sit up and eat some of my game, so that you may give me your blessing."

20 Isaac asked his son, "How did you find it so quickly, my son?"

"The Homeboy, The Big Gangster gave me success," he replied.

21 Then Isaac said to Jacob, "Come near so I can touch you, my son, to know whether you really are my son Esau or not."

22 Jacob went close to his father Isaac, who touched him and said, "The voice is the voice of Jacob, but the hands are the hands of Esau." 23 He did not recognize him, for his hands were hairy like those of his brother Esau; so he proceeded to bless him. 24 "Are you really my son Esau?" he asked.

"I am," he replied.

25 Then he said, "My son, bring me some of your game to eat, so that I may give you my blessing."

Jacob brought it to him and he ate; and he brought some malt liquor and he drank. 26 Then his father Isaac said to him, "Come here, my son, and kiss me."

27 So he went to him and kissed him. When Isaac caught the smell of his clothes, he blessed him and said,

> "Ah, the smell of my son
>   is like the smell of a field
>   that the Homeboy has blessed.
> 28 May The Big Gangster give you heaven's dew
>   and earth's richness—
>   an abundance of grain and new malt liquor.
> 29 May nations serve you
>   and peoples bow down to you.

> Be Homeboy over your brothers,
>> and may the sons of your mother bow down to you.
> May those who curse you be cursed
>> and those who bless you be blessed."

30 After Isaac finished blessing him, and Jacob had scarcely left his father's presence, his brother Esau came in from hunting. 31 He too prepared some tasty food and brought it to his father. Then he said to him, "My father, please sit up and eat some of my game, so that you may give me your blessing."

32 His father Isaac asked him, "Who are you?"

"I am your son," he answered, "your firstborn, Esau."

33 Isaac trembled violently and said, "Who was it, then, that hunted game and brought it to me? I ate it just before you came and I blessed him—and indeed he will be blessed!"

34 When Esau heard his father's words, he burst out with a loud and bitter cry and said to his father, "Bless me—me too, my father!"

35 But he said, "Your brother came deceitfully and took your blessing."

36 Esau said, "Isn't he rightly named Jacob? This is the second time he has taken advantage of me: He took my birthright, and now he's taken my blessing!" Then he asked, "Haven't you reserved any blessing for me?"

37 Isaac answered Esau, "I have made him Homeboy over you and have made all his relatives his servants, and I have sustained him with grain and new malt liquor. So what can I possibly do for you, my son?"

38 Esau said to his father, "Do you have only one blessing, my father? Bless me too, my father!" Then Esau wept aloud.

39 His father Isaac answered him,
> "Your dwelling will be
>> away from the earth's richness,
>> away from the dew of heaven above.
> 40 You will live by the sword
>> and you will serve your brother.

But when you grow restless,
you will throw his yoke
from off your neck."

41 Esau held a grudge against Jacob because of the blessing his father had given him. He said to himself, "The days of mourning for my father are near; then I will kill my brother Jacob."

42 When Rebekah was told what her older son Esau had said, she sent for her younger son Jacob and said to him, "Your brother Esau is planning to avenge himself by killing you. 43 Now then, my son, do what I say: Flee at once to my brother Laban in Harran. 44 Stay with him for a while until your brother's fury subsides. 45 When your brother is no longer angry with you and forgets what you did to him, I'll send word for you to come back from there. Why should I lose both of you in one day?"

46 Then Rebekah said to Isaac, "I'm disgusted with living because of these Hittite women. If Jacob takes a wife from among the women of this land, from Hittite women like these, my life will not be worth living."

28 So Isaac called for Jacob and blessed him. Then he commanded him: "Do not marry a Canaanite woman. 2 Go at once to Paddan Aram, to the house of your mother's father Bethuel. Take a wife for yourself there, from among the daughters of Laban, your mother's brother. 3 May The Big Gangster Almighty bless you and make you fruitful and increase your numbers until you become a community of peoples. 4 May he give you and your descendants the blessing given to Abraham, so that you may take possession of the land where you now reside as a foreigner, the land The Big Gangster gave to Abraham." 5 Then Isaac sent Jacob on his way, and he went to Paddan Aram, to Laban son of Bethuel the Aramean, the brother of Rebekah, who was the mother of Jacob and Esau.

6 Now Esau learned that Isaac had blessed Jacob and had sent him to Paddan Aram to take a wife from there, and that when he blessed him he commanded him, "Do not marry a Canaanite woman," 7 and that Jacob had obeyed his father and mother and had gone to Paddan Aram. 8 Esau then realized how

displeasing the Canaanite women were to his father Isaac; 9 so he went to Ishmael and married Mahalath, the sister of Nebaioth and daughter of Ishmael son of Abraham, in addition to the wives he already had.

Jacob's Dream at Bethel

10 Jacob left Beersheba and set out for Harran. 11 When he reached a certain place, he stopped for the night because the sun had set. Taking one of the stones there, he put it under his head and lay down to sleep. 12 He had a dream in which he saw a stairway resting on the earth, with its top reaching to heaven, and the angels of The Big Gangster were ascending and descending on it. 13 There above it stood the Holy Homeboy, and he said: "I am the Homeboy, The Big Gangster of your father Abraham and The Big Gangster of Isaac. I will give you and your descendants the land on which you are lying. 14 Your descendants will be like the dust of the earth, and you will spread out to the west and to the east, to the north and to the south. All peoples on earth will be blessed through you and your offspring. 15 I am with you and will watch over you wherever you go, and I will bring you back to this land. I will not leave you until I have done what I have promised you."

16 When Jacob awoke from his sleep, he thought, "Surely the Homeboy is in this place, and I was not aware of it." 17 He was afraid and said, "How awesome is this place! This is none other than the house of The Big Gangster; this is the gate of heaven."

18 Early the next morning Jacob took the stone he had placed under his head and set it up as a pillar and poured oil on top of it. 19 He called that place Bethel, though the city used to be called Luz.

20 Then Jacob made a vow, saying, "If The Big Gangster will be with me and will watch over me on this journey I am taking and will give me food to eat and clothes to wear 21 so that I return safely to my father's household, then the Homeboy will be The Big Gangster 22 and this stone that I have set up as a pillar will be The Big Gangster's house, and of all that you give me I will give you a tenth."

Jacob Arrives in Paddan Aram

29 Then Jacob continued on his journey and came to the land of the eastern peoples. 2 There he saw a well in the open country, with three flocks of sheep lying near it because the flocks were watered from that well. The stone over the mouth of the well was large. 3 When all the flocks were gathered there, the shepherds would roll the stone away from the well's mouth and water the sheep. Then they would return the stone to its place over the mouth of the well.

4 Jacob asked the shepherds, "My brothers, where are you from?"

"We're from Harran," they replied.

5 He said to them, "Do you know Laban, Nahor's grandson?"

"Yes, we know him," they answered.

6 Then Jacob asked them, "Is he well?"

"Yes, he is," they said, "and here comes his daughter Rachel with the sheep."

7 "Look," he said, "the sun is still high; it is not time for the flocks to be gathered. Water the sheep and take them back to pasture."

8 "We can't," they replied, "until all the flocks are gathered and the stone has been rolled away from the mouth of the well. Then we will water the sheep."

9 While he was still talking with them, Rachel came with her father's sheep, for she was a shepherd. 10 When Jacob saw Rachel daughter of his uncle Laban, and Laban's sheep, he went over and rolled the stone away from the mouth of the well and watered his uncle's sheep. 11 Then Jacob kissed Rachel and began to weep aloud. 12 He had told Rachel that he was a relative of her father and a son of Rebekah. So she ran and told her father.

13 As soon as Laban heard the news about Jacob, his sister's son, he hurried to meet him. He embraced him and kissed him and brought him to his home, and there Jacob told him all these things. 14 Then Laban said to him, "You are my own flesh and blood."

Jacob Marries Leah and Rachel

After Jacob had stayed with him for a whole month, 15 Laban said to him, "Just because you are a relative of mine, should you work for me for nothing? Tell me what your wages should be."

16 Now Laban had two daughters; the name of the older was Leah, and the name of the younger was Rachel. 17 Leah had weak eyes, but Rachel had a lovely figure and was beautiful. 18 Jacob was in love with Rachel and said, "I'll work for you seven years in return for your younger daughter Rachel."

19 Laban said, "It's better that I give her to you than to some other man. Stay here with me." 20 So Jacob served seven years to get Rachel, but they seemed like only a few days to him because of his love for her.

21 Then Jacob said to Laban, "Give me my wife. My time is completed, and I want to make love to her."

22 So Laban brought together all the people of the place and gave a feast. 23 But when evening came, he took his daughter Leah and brought her to Jacob, and Jacob made love to her. 24 And Laban gave his servant Zilpah to his daughter as her attendant.

25 When morning came, there was Leah! So Jacob said to Laban, "What is this you have done to me? I served you for Rachel, didn't I? Why have you deceived me?"

26 Laban replied, "It is not our custom here to give the younger daughter in marriage before the older one. 27 Finish this daughter's bridal week; then we will give you the younger one also, in return for another seven years of work."

28 And Jacob did so. He finished the week with Leah, and then Laban gave him his daughter Rachel to be his wife. 29 Laban gave his servant Bilhah to his daughter Rachel as her attendant. 30 Jacob made love to Rachel also, and his love for Rachel was greater than his love for Leah. And he worked for Laban another seven years.

Jacob's Children

31 When the Homeboy saw that Leah was not loved, he enabled her to conceive, but Rachel remained childless. 32

Leah became pregnant and gave birth to a son. She named him Reuben, for she said, "It is because the Homeboy has seen my misery. Surely my husband will love me now."

33 She conceived again, and when she gave birth to a son she said, "Because the Homeboy heard that I am not loved, he gave me this one too." So she named him Simeon.

34 Again she conceived, and when she gave birth to a son she said, "Now at last my husband will become attached to me, because I have borne him three sons." So he was named Levi.

35 She conceived again, and when she gave birth to a son she said, "This time I will praise the Homeboy." So she named him Judah. Then she stopped having children.

30 When Rachel saw that she was not bearing Jacob any children, she became jealous of her sister. So she said to Jacob, "Give me children, or I'll die!"

2 Jacob became angry with her and said, "Am I in the place of The Big Gangster, who has kept you from having children?"

3 Then she said, "Here is Bilhah, my servant. Sleep with her so that she can bear children for me and I too can build a family through her."

4 So she gave him her servant Bilhah as a wife. Jacob slept with her, 5 and she became pregnant and bore him a son. 6 Then Rachel said, "The Big Gangster has vindicated me; he has listened to my plea and given me a son." Because of this she named him Dan.

7 Rachel's servant Bilhah conceived again and bore Jacob a second son. 8 Then Rachel said, "I have had a great struggle with my sister, and I have won." So she named him Naphtali.

9 When Leah saw that she had stopped having children, she took her servant Zilpah and gave her to Jacob as a wife. 10 Leah's servant Zilpah bore Jacob a son. 11 Then Leah said, "What good fortune!"So she named him Gad.

12 Leah's servant Zilpah bore Jacob a second son. 13 Then Leah said, "How happy I am! The women will call me happy." So she named him Asher.

14 During wheat harvest, Reuben went out into the fields and found some mandrake plants, which he brought to his mother

Leah. Rachel said to Leah, "Please give me some of your son's mandrakes."

15 But she said to her, "Wasn't it enough that you took away my husband? Will you take my son's mandrakes too?"

"Very well," Rachel said, "he can sleep with you tonight in return for your son's mandrakes."

16 So when Jacob came in from the fields that evening, Leah went out to meet him. "You must sleep with me," she said. "I have hired you with my son's mandrakes." So he slept with her that night.

17 The Big Gangster listened to Leah, and she became pregnant and bore Jacob a fifth son. 18 Then Leah said, "The Big Gangster has rewarded me for giving my servant to my husband." So she named him Issachar.[

19 Leah conceived again and bore Jacob a sixth son. 20 Then Leah said, "The Big Gangster has presented me with a precious gift. This time my husband will treat me with honor, because I have borne him six sons." So she named him Zebulun.

21 Sometime later she gave birth to a daughter and named her Dinah.

22 Then The Big Gangster remembered Rachel; he listened to her and enabled her to conceive. 23 She became pregnant and gave birth to a son and said, "The Big Gangster has taken away my disgrace." 24 She named him Joseph, and said, "May the Homeboy add to me another son."

Jacob's Flocks Increase

25 After Rachel gave birth to Joseph, Jacob said to Laban, "Send me on my way so I can go back to my own homeland. 26 Give me my wives and children, for whom I have served you, and I will be on my way. You know how much work I've done for you."

27 But Laban said to him, "If I have found favor in your eyes, please stay. I have learned by divination that the Homeboy has blessed me because of you." 28 He added, "Name your wages, and I will pay them."

29 Jacob said to him, "You know how I have worked for you and how your livestock has fared under my care. 30 The little

you had before I came has increased greatly, and the Homeboy has blessed you wherever I have been. But now, when may I do something for my own household?"

31 "What shall I give you?" he asked.

"Don't give me anything," Jacob replied. "But if you will do this one thing for me, I will go on tending your flocks and watching over them: 32 Let me go through all your flocks today and remove from them every speckled or spotted sheep, every dark-colored lamb and every spotted or speckled goat. They will be my wages. 33 And my honesty will testify for me in the future, whenever you check on the wages you have paid me. Any goat in my possession that is not speckled or spotted, or any lamb that is not dark-colored, will be considered stolen."

34 "Agreed," said Laban. "Let it be as you have said." 35 That same day he removed all the male goats that were streaked or spotted, and all the speckled or spotted female goats (all that had white on them) and all the dark-colored lambs, and he placed them in the care of his sons. 36 Then he put a three-day journey between himself and Jacob, while Jacob continued to tend the rest of Laban's flocks.

37 Jacob, however, took fresh-cut branches from poplar, almond and plane trees and made white stripes on them by peeling the bark and exposing the white inner wood of the branches. 38 Then he placed the peeled branches in all the watering troughs, so that they would be directly in front of the flocks when they came to drink. When the flocks were in heat and came to drink, 39 they mated in front of the branches. And they bore young that were streaked or speckled or spotted. 40 Jacob set apart the young of the flock by themselves, but made the rest face the streaked and dark-colored animals that belonged to Laban. Thus he made separate flocks for himself and did not put them with Laban's animals. 41 Whenever the stronger females were in heat, Jacob would place the branches in the troughs in front of the animals so they would mate near the branches, 42 but if the animals were weak, he would not place them there. So the weak animals went to Laban and the strong ones to Jacob. 43 In this way the man grew exceedingly prosperous and came to

own large flocks, and female and male servants, and camels and donkeys.

Jacob Flees From Laban

31 Jacob heard that Laban's sons were saying, "Jacob has taken everything our father owned and has gained all this wealth from what belonged to our father." 2 And Jacob noticed that Laban's attitude toward him was not what it had been.

3 Then the Homeboy said to Jacob, "Go back to the land of your fathers and to your relatives, and I will be with you."

4 So Jacob sent word to Rachel and Leah to come out to the fields where his flocks were. 5 He said to them, "I see that your father's attitude toward me is not what it was before, but The Big Gangster of my father has been with me. 6 You know that I've worked for your father with all my strength, 7 yet your father has cheated me by changing my wages ten times. However, The Big Gangster has not allowed him to harm me. 8 If he said, 'The speckled ones will be your wages,' then all the flocks gave birth to speckled young; and if he said, 'The streaked ones will be your wages,' then all the flocks bore streaked young. 9 So The Big Gangster has taken away your father's livestock and has given them to me.

10 "In breeding season I once had a dream in which I looked up and saw that the male goats mating with the flock were streaked, speckled or spotted. 11 The angel of The Big Gangster said to me in the dream, 'Jacob.' I answered, 'Here I am.' 12 And he said, 'Look up and see that all the male goats mating with the flock are streaked, speckled or spotted, for I have seen all that Laban has been doing to you. 13 I am The Big Gangster of Bethel, where you anointed a pillar and where you made a vow to me. Now leave this land at once and go back to your native land.'"

14 Then Rachel and Leah replied, "Do we still have any share in the inheritance of our father's estate? 15 Does he not regard us as foreigners? Not only has he sold us, but he has used up what was paid for us. 16 Surely all the wealth that The Big Gangster

took away from our father belongs to us and our children. So do whatever The Big Gangster has told you." 17 Then Jacob put his children and his wives on camels, 18 and he drove all his livestock ahead of him, along with all the goods he had accumulated in Paddan Aram, to go to his father Isaac in the land of Canaan.

19 When Laban had gone to shear his sheep, Rachel stole her father's household religious idol. 20 Moreover, Jacob deceived Laban the Aramean by not telling him he was running away. 21 So he fled with all he had, crossed the Euphrates River, and headed for the hill country of Gilead.

Laban Pursues Jacob

22 On the third day Laban was told that Jacob had fled. 23 Taking his relatives with him, he pursued Jacob for seven days and caught up with him in the hill country of Gilead. 24 Then The Big Gangster came to Laban the Aramean in a dream at night and said to him, "Be careful not to say anything to Jacob, either good or bad."

25 Jacob had pitched his tent in the hill country of Gilead when Laban overtook him, and Laban and his relatives camped there too. 26 Then Laban said to Jacob, "What have you done? You've deceived me, and you've carried off my daughters like captives in war. 27 Why did you run off secretly and deceive me? Why didn't you tell me, so I could send you away with joy and singing to the music of timbrels and harps? 28 You didn't even let me kiss my grandchildren and my daughters goodbye. You have done a foolish thing. 29 I have the power to harm you; but last night The Big Gangster of your father said to me, 'Be careful not to say anything to Jacob, either good or bad.' 30 Now you have gone off because you longed to return to your father's household. But why did you steal my religious idols?"

31 Jacob answered Laban, "I was afraid, because I thought you would take your daughters away from me by force. 32 But if you find anyone who has your religious idols, that person shall not live. In the presence of our relatives, see for yourself whether there is anything of yours here with me; and if so, take it." Now Jacob did not know that Rachel had stolen the religious idols.

33 So Laban went into Jacob's tent and into Leah's tent and into the tent of the two female servants, but he found nothing. After he came out of Leah's tent, he entered Rachel's tent. 34 Now Rachel had taken the household religious idols and put them inside her camel's saddle and was sitting on them. Laban searched through everything in the tent but found nothing.

35 Rachel said to her father, "Don't be angry that I cannot stand up in your presence; I'm having my menstrual period." So he searched but could not find the household religious idols.

36 Jacob was angry and took Laban to task. "What is my crime?" he asked Laban. "How have I wronged you that you hunt me down? 37 Now that you have searched through all my goods, what have you found that belongs to your household? Put it here in front of your relatives and mine, and let them judge between the two of us.

38 "I have been with you for twenty years now. Your sheep and goats have not miscarried, nor have I eaten rams from your flocks. 39 I did not bring you animals torn by wild beasts; I bore the loss myself. And you demanded payment from me for whatever was stolen by day or night. 40 This was my situation: The heat consumed me in the daytime and the cold at night, and sleep fled from my eyes. 41 It was like this for the twenty years I was in your household. I worked for you fourteen years for your two daughters and six years for your flocks, and you changed my wages ten times. 42 If The Big Gangster of my father,The Big Gangster of Abraham and the Fear of Isaac, had not been with me, you would surely have sent me away empty-handed. But The Big Gangster has seen my hardship and the toil of my hands, and last night he rebuked you."

43 Laban answered Jacob, "The women are my daughters, the children are my children, and the flocks are my flocks. All you see is mine. Yet what can I do today about these daughters of mine, or about the children they have borne? 44 Come now, let's make a covenant, you and I, and let it serve as a witness between us."

45 So Jacob took a stone and set it up as a pillar. 46 He said to his relatives, "Gather some stones." So they took stones and

piled them in a heap, and they ate there by the heap. 47 Laban called it Jegar Sahadutha, and Jacob called it Galeed.

48 Laban said, "This heap is a witness between you and me today." That is why it was called Galeed. 49 It was also called Mizpah, because he said, "May the Homeboy keep watch between you and me when we are away from each other. 50 If you mistreat my daughters or if you take any wives besides my daughters, even though no one is with us, remember that The Big Gangster is a witness between you and me."

51 Laban also said to Jacob, "Here is this heap, and here is this pillar I have set up between you and me. 52 This heap is a witness, and this pillar is a witness, that I will not go past this heap to your side to harm you and that you will not go past this heap and pillar to my side to harm me. 53 May The Big Gangster of Abraham and The Big Gangster of Nahor, The Big Gangster of their father, judge between us."

So Jacob took an oath in the name of the Fear of his father Isaac. 54 He offered a sacrifice there in the hill country and invited his relatives to a meal. After they had eaten, they spent the night there.

55 Early the next morning Laban kissed his grandchildren and his daughters and blessed them. Then he left and returned home.

Jacob Prepares to Meet Esau

32 Jacob also went on his way, and the angels of The Big Gangster met him. 2 When Jacob saw them, he said, "This is the camp of The Big Gangster!" So he named that place Mahanaim.

3 Jacob sent messengers ahead of him to his brother Esau in the land of Seir, the country of Edom. 4 He instructed them: "This is what you are to say to my brother Esau: 'Your servant Jacob says, I have been staying with Laban and have remained there till now. 5 I have cattle and donkeys, sheep and goats, male and female servants. Now I am sending this message to you, that I may find favor in your eyes.'"

6 When the messengers returned to Jacob, they said, "We went to your brother Esau, and now he is coming to meet you, and four hundred men are with him."

7 In great fear and distress Jacob divided the people who were with him into two groups, and the flocks and herds and camels as well. 8 He thought, "If Esau comes and attacks one group, the group that is left may escape."

9 Then Jacob prayed, "O The Big Gangster of my father Abraham, The Big Gangster of my father Isaac, Homeboy, you who said to me, 'Go back to your country and your relatives, and I will make you prosper,' 10 I am unworthy of all the kindness and faithfulness you have shown your servant. I had only my staff when I crossed this Jordan, but now I have become two camps. 11 Save me, I pray, from the hand of my brother Esau, for I am afraid he will come and attack me, and also the mothers with their children. 12 But you have said, 'I will surely make you prosper and will make your descendants like the sand of the sea, which cannot be counted.'"

13 He spent the night there, and from what he had with him he selected a gift for his brother Esau: 14 two hundred female goats and twenty male goats, two hundred ewes and twenty rams, 15 thirty female camels with their young, forty cows and ten bulls, and twenty female donkeys and ten male donkeys. 16 He put them in the care of his servants, each herd by itself, and said to his servants, "Go ahead of me, and keep some space between the herds."

17 He instructed the one in the lead: "When my brother Esau meets you and asks, 'Who do you belong to, and where are you going, and who owns all these animals in front of you?' 18 then you are to say, 'They belong to your servant Jacob. They are a gift sent to my brother Esau, and he is coming behind us.'"

19 He also instructed the second, the third and all the others who followed the herds: "You are to say the same thing to Esau when you meet him. 20 And be sure to say, 'Your servant Jacob is coming behind us.'" For he thought, "I will pacify him with these gifts I am sending on ahead; later, when I see him, perhaps he will receive me." 21 So Jacob's gifts went on ahead of him, but he himself spent the night in the camp.

Jacob Wrestles With The Big Gangster

22 That night Jacob got up and took his two wives, his two female servants and his eleven sons and crossed the ford of the Jabbok. 23 After he had sent them across the stream, he sent over all his possessions. 24 So Jacob was left alone, and a man wrestled with him till daybreak. 25 When the man saw that he could not overpower him, he touched the socket of Jacob's hip so that his hip was wrenched as he wrestled with the man. 26 Then the man said, "Let me go, for it is daybreak."

But Jacob replied, "I will not let you go unless you bless me."

27 The man asked him, "What is your name?"

"Jacob," he answered.

28 Then the man said, "Your name will no longer be Jacob, but Israel, because you have struggled with The Big Gangster and with humans and have overcome."

29 Jacob said, "Please tell me your name."

But he replied, "Why do you ask my name?" Then he blessed him there.

30 So Jacob called the place Peniel, saying, "It is because I saw The Big Gangster face to face, and yet my life was spared."

31 The sun rose above him as he passed Peniel, and he was limping because of his hip. 32 Therefore to this day the Israelites do not eat the tendon attached to the socket of the hip, because the socket of Jacob's hip was touched near the tendon.

Jacob Meets Esau

33 Jacob looked up and there was Esau, coming with his four hundred men; so he divided the children among Leah, Rachel and the two female servants. 2 He put the female servants and their children in front, Leah and her children next, and Rachel and Joseph in the rear. 3 He himself went on ahead and bowed down to the ground seven times as he approached his brother.

4 But Esau ran to meet Jacob and embraced him; he threw his arms around his neck and kissed him. And they wept. 5 Then

Esau looked up and saw the women and children. "Who are these with you?" he asked.

Jacob answered, "They are the children The Big Gangster has graciously given your servant."

6 Then the female servants and their children approached and bowed down. 7 Next, Leah and her children came and bowed down. Last of all came Joseph and Rachel, and they too bowed down.

8 Esau asked, "What's the meaning of all these flocks and herds I met?"

"To find favor in your eyes, my brother," he said.

9 But Esau said, "I already have plenty, my brother. Keep what you have for yourself."

10 "No, please!" said Jacob. "If I have found favor in your eyes, accept this gift from me. For to see your face is like seeing the face of The Big Gangster, now that you have received me favorably. 11 Please accept the present that was brought to you, for The Big Gangster has been gracious to me and I have all I need." And because Jacob insisted, Esau accepted it.

12 Then Esau said, "Let us be on our way; I'll accompany you."

13 But Jacob said to him, "You know that the children are tender and that I must care for the ewes and cows that are nursing their young. If they are driven hard just one day, all the animals will die. 14 So let my brother go on ahead of his servant, while I move along slowly at the pace of the flocks and herds before me and the pace of the children, until I come to my brother in Seir."

15 Esau said, "Then let me leave some of my men with you."

"But why do that?" Jacob asked. "Just let me find favor in the eyes of my brother."

16 So that day Esau started on his way back to Seir. 17 Jacob, however, went to Sukkoth, where he built a place for himself and made shelters for his livestock. That is why the place is called Sukkoth.

18 After Jacob came from Paddan Aram, he arrived safely at the city of Shechem in Canaan and camped within sight of the city. 19 For a hundred pieces of silver, he bought from the sons

of Hamor, the father of Shechem, the plot of ground where he pitched his tent. 20 There he set up an altar and called it El Elohe Israel.

Dinah and the Shechemites

34 Now Dinah, the daughter Leah had borne to Jacob, went out to visit the women of the land. 2 When Shechem son of Hamor the Hivite, the ruler of that area, saw her, he took her and raped her. 3 His heart was drawn to Dinah daughter of Jacob; he loved the young woman and spoke tenderly to her. 4 And Shechem said to his father Hamor, "Get me this girl as my wife."

5 When Jacob heard that his daughter Dinah had been defiled, his sons were in the fields with his livestock; so he did nothing about it until they came home.

6 Then Shechem's father Hamor went out to talk with Jacob. 7 Meanwhile, Jacob's sons had come in from the fields as soon as they heard what had happened. They were shocked and furious, because Shechem had done an outrageous thing in Israel by sleeping with Jacob's daughter—a thing that should not be done.

8 But Hamor said to them, "My son Shechem has his heart set on your daughter. Please give her to him as his wife. 9 Intermarry with us; give us your daughters and take our daughters for yourselves. 10 You can settle among us; the land is open to you. Live in it, trade in it, and acquire property in it."

11 Then Shechem said to Dinah's father and brothers, "Let me find favor in your eyes, and I will give you whatever you ask. 12 Make the price for the bride and the gift I am to bring as great as you like, and I'll pay whatever you ask me. Only give me the young woman as my wife."

13 Because their sister Dinah had been defiled, Jacob's sons replied deceitfully as they spoke to Shechem and his father Hamor. 14 They said to them, "We can't do such a thing; we can't give our sister to a man who is not circumcised. That would be a disgrace to us. 15 We will enter into an agreement with you on one condition only: that you become like us by circumcising all your males. 16 Then we will give you our daughters and take your daughters for ourselves. We'll settle among you and

become one people with you. 17 But if you will not agree to be circumcised, we'll take our sister and go."

18 Their proposal seemed good to Hamor and his son Shechem. 19 The young man, who was the most honored of all his father's family, lost no time in doing what they said, because he was delighted with Jacob's daughter. 20 So Hamor and his son Shechem went to the gate of their city to speak to the men of their city. 21 "These men are friendly toward us," they said. "Let them live in our land and trade in it; the land has plenty of room for them. We can marry their daughters and they can marry ours. 22 But the men will agree to live with us as one people only on the condition that our males be circumcised, as they themselves are. 23 Won't their livestock, their property and all their other animals become ours? So let us agree to their terms, and they will settle among us."

24 All the men who went out of the city gate agreed with Hamor and his son Shechem, and every male in the city was circumcised.

25 Three days later, while all of them were still in pain, two of Jacob's sons, Simeon and Levi, Dinah's brothers, took their swords and attacked the unsuspecting city, killing every male. 26 They put Hamor and his son Shechem to the sword and took Dinah from Shechem's house and left. 27 The sons of Jacob came upon the dead bodies and looted the city where their sister had been defiled. 28 They seized their flocks and herds and donkeys and everything else of theirs in the city and out in the fields. 29 They carried off all their wealth and all their women and children, taking as plunder everything in the houses.

30 Then Jacob said to Simeon and Levi, "You have brought trouble on me by making me obnoxious to the Canaanites and Perizzites, the people living in this land. We are few in number, and if they join forces against me and attack me, I and my household will be destroyed."

31 But they replied, "Should he have treated our sister like a prostitute?"

Jacob Returns to Bethel

35 Then The Big Gangster said to Jacob, "Go up to Bethel and settle there, and build an altar there to The Big Gangster, who appeared to you when you were fleeing from your brother Esau."

2 So Jacob said to his household and to all who were with him, "Get rid of the foreign religious idols you have with you, and purify yourselves and change your clothes. 3 Then come, let us go up to Bethel, where I will build an altar to The Big Gangster, who answered me in the day of my distress and who has been with me wherever I have gone." 4 So they gave Jacob all the foreign the Big Gangsters they had and the rings in their ears, and Jacob buried them under the oak at Shechem. 5 Then they set out, and the terror of The Big Gangster fell on the towns all around them so that no one pursued them.

6 Jacob and all the people with him came to Luz (that is, Bethel) in the land of Canaan. 7 There he built an altar, and he called the place El Bethel, because it was there that The Big Gangster revealed himself to him when he was fleeing from his brother.

8 Now Deborah, Rebekah's nurse, died and was buried under the oak outside Bethel. So it was named Allon Bakuth.

9 After Jacob returned from Paddan Aram, The Big Gangster appeared to him again and blessed him. 10 The Big Gangster said to him, "Your name is Jacob, but you will no longer be called Jacob; your name will be Israel." So he named him Israel.

11 And The Big Gangster said to him, "I am The Big Gangster Almighty; be fruitful and increase in number. A nation and a community of nations will come from you, and kings will be among your descendants. 12 The land I gave to Abraham and Isaac I also give to you, and I will give this land to your descendants after you." 13 Then The Big Gangster went up from him at the place where he had talked with him.

14 Jacob set up a stone pillar at the place where The Big Gangster had talked with him, and he poured out a drink offering on it; he also poured oil on it. 15 Jacob called the place where The Big Gangster had talked with him Bethel.

The Deaths of Rachel and Isaac

16 Then they moved on from Bethel. While they were still some distance from Ephrath, Rachel began to give birth and had great difficulty. 17 And as she was having great difficulty in childbirth, the midwife said to her, "Don't despair, for you have another son." 18 As she breathed her last—for she was dying—she named her son Ben-Oni. But his father named him Benjamin.

19 So Rachel died and was buried on the way to Ephrath (that is, Bethlehem). 20 Over her tomb Jacob set up a pillar, and to this day that pillar marks Rachel's tomb.

21 Israel moved on again and pitched his tent beyond Migdal Eder. 22 While Israel was living in that region, Reuben went in and slept with his father's concubine Bilhah, and Israel heard of it.

Jacob had twelve sons:
23 The sons of Leah:
Reuben the firstborn of Jacob,
Simeon, Levi, Judah, Issachar and Zebulun.
24 The sons of Rachel:
Joseph and Benjamin.
25 The sons of Rachel's servant Bilhah:
Dan and Naphtali.
26 The sons of Leah's servant Zilpah:
Gad and Asher.
These were the sons of Jacob, who were born to him in Paddan Aram.

27 Jacob came home to his father Isaac in Mamre, near Kiriath Arba (that is, Hebron), where Abraham and Isaac had stayed. 28 Isaac lived a hundred and eighty years. 29 Then he breathed his last and died and was gathered to his people, old and full of years. And his sons Esau and Jacob buried him.

Esau's Descendants

36 This is the account of the family line of Esau (that is, Edom).

2 Esau took his wives from the women of Canaan: Adah daughter of Elon the Hittite, and Oholibamah daughter of Anah and granddaughter of Zibeon the Hivite— 3 also Basemath daughter of Ishmael and sister of Nebaioth.

4 Adah bore Eliphaz to Esau, Basemath bore Reuel, 5 and Oholibamah bore Jeush, Jalam and Korah. These were the sons of Esau, who were born to him in Canaan.

6 Esau took his wives and sons and daughters and all the members of his household, as well as his livestock and all his other animals and all the goods he had acquired in Canaan, and moved to a land some distance from his brother Jacob. 7 Their possessions were too great for them to remain together; the land where they were staying could not support them both because of their livestock. 8 So Esau (that is, Edom) settled in the hill country of Seir.

9 This is the account of the family line of Esau the father of the Edomites in the hill country of Seir.

10 These are the names of Esau's sons:

Eliphaz, the son of Esau's wife Adah, and Reuel, the son of Esau's wife Basemath.

11 The sons of Eliphaz:

Teman, Omar, Zepho, Gatam and Kenaz.

12 Esau's son Eliphaz also had a concubine named Timna, who bore him Amalek. These were grandsons of Esau's wife Adah.

13 The sons of Reuel:

Nahath, Zerah, Shammah and Mizzah. These were grandsons of Esau's wife Basemath.

14 The sons of Esau's wife Oholibamah daughter of Anah and granddaughter of Zibeon, whom she bore to Esau:

Jeush, Jalam and Korah.

15 These were the chiefs among Esau's descendants:

The sons of Eliphaz the firstborn of Esau:

Chiefs Teman, Omar, Zepho, Kenaz, 16 Korah, Gatam and Amalek. These were the chiefs descended from Eliphaz in Edom; they were grandsons of Adah.

17 The sons of Esau's son Reuel:
Chiefs Nahath, Zerah, Shammah and Mizzah. These were the chiefs descended from Reuel in Edom; they were grandsons of Esau's wife Basemath.
18 The sons of Esau's wife Oholibamah:
Chiefs Jeush, Jalam and Korah. These were the chiefs descended from Esau's wife Oholibamah daughter of Anah.
19 These were the sons of Esau (that is, Edom), and these were their chiefs.
20 These were the sons of Seir the Horite, who were living in the region:
Lotan, Shobal, Zibeon, Anah, 21 Dishon, Ezer and Dishan. These sons of Seir in Edom were Horite chiefs.
22 The sons of Lotan:
Hori and Homam. Timna was Lotan's sister.
23 The sons of Shobal:
Alvan, Manahath, Ebal, Shepho and Onam.
24 The sons of Zibeon:
Aiah and Anah. This is the Anah who discovered the hot springs in the desert while he was grazing the donkeys of his father Zibeon.
25 The children of Anah:
Dishon and Oholibamah daughter of Anah.
26 The sons of Dishon:
Hemdan, Eshban, Ithran and Keran.
27 The sons of Ezer:
Bilhan, Zaavan and Akan.
28 The sons of Dishan:
Uz and Aran.
29 These were the Horite chiefs:
Lotan, Shobal, Zibeon, Anah, 30 Dishon, Ezer and Dishan. These were the Horite chiefs, according to their divisions, in the land of Seir.

The Rulers of Edom

31 These were the kings who reigned in Edom before any Israelite king reigned:

32 Bela son of Beor became king of Edom. His city was named Dinhabah.

33 When Bela died, Jobab son of Zerah from Bozrah succeeded him as king.

34 When Jobab died, Husham from the land of the Temanites succeeded him as king.

35 When Husham died, Hadad son of Bedad, who defeated Midian in the country of Moab, succeeded him as king. His city was named Avith.

36 When Hadad died, Samlah from Masrekah succeeded him as king.

37 When Samlah died, Shaul from Rehoboth on the river succeeded him as king.

38 When Shaul died, Baal-Hanan son of Akbor succeeded him as king.

39 When Baal-Hanan son of Akbor died, Hadad succeeded him as king. His city was named Pau, and his wife's name was Mehetabel daughter of Matred, the daughter of Me-Zahab.

40 These were the chiefs descended from Esau, by name, according to their clans and regions:

Timna, Alvah, Jetheth, 41 Oholibamah, Elah, Pinon, 42 Kenaz, Teman, Mibzar, 43 Magdiel and Iram. These were the chiefs of Edom, according to their settlements in the land they occupied.

This is the family line of Esau, the father of the Edomites.

Joseph's Dreams

37 Jacob lived in the land where his father had stayed, the land of Canaan.

2 This is the account of Jacob's family line.

Joseph, a young man of seventeen, was tending the flocks with his brothers, the sons of Bilhah and the sons of Zilpah, his father's wives, and he brought their father a bad report about them.

3 Now Israel loved Joseph more than any of his other sons, because he had been born to him in his old age; and he made an ornate robe for him. 4 When his brothers saw that their father

loved him more than any of them, they hated him and could not speak a kind word to him.
5 Joseph had a dream, and when he told it to his brothers, they hated him all the more. 6 He said to them, "Listen to this dream I had: 7 We were binding sheaves of grain out in the field when suddenly my sheaf rose and stood upright, while your sheaves gathered around mine and bowed down to it."
8 His brothers said to him, "Do you intend to reign over us? Will you actually rule us?" And they hated him all the more because of his dream and what he had said.
9 Then he had another dream, and he told it to his brothers. "Listen," he said, "I had another dream, and this time the sun and moon and eleven stars were bowing down to me."
10 When he told his father as well as his brothers, his father rebuked him and said, "What is this dream you had? Will your mother and I and your brothers actually come and bow down to the ground before you?" 11 His brothers were jealous of him, but his father kept the matter in mind.

Joseph Sold by His Brothers

12 Now his brothers had gone to graze their father's flocks near Shechem, 13 and Israel said to Joseph, "As you know, your brothers are grazing the flocks near Shechem. Come, I am going to send you to them."
"Very well," he replied.
14 So he said to him, "Go and see if all is well with your brothers and with the flocks, and bring word back to me." Then he sent him off from the Valley of Hebron.
When Joseph arrived at Shechem, 15 a man found him wandering around in the fields and asked him, "What are you looking for?"
16 He replied, "I'm looking for my brothers. Can you tell me where they are grazing their flocks?"
17 "They have moved on from here," the man answered. "I heard them say, 'Let's go to Dothan.'"
So Joseph went after his brothers and found them near Dothan. 18 But they saw him in the distance, and before he reached them, they plotted to kill him.

19 "Here comes that dreamer!" they said to each other. 20 "Come now, let's kill him and throw him into one of these cisterns and say that a ferocious animal devoured him. Then we'll see what comes of his dreams."

21 When Reuben heard this, he tried to rescue him from their hands. "Let's not take his life," he said. 22 "Don't shed any blood. Throw him into this cistern here in the wilderness, but don't lay a hand on him." Reuben said this to rescue him from them and take him back to his father.

23 So when Joseph came to his brothers, they stripped him of his robe—the ornate robe he was wearing— 24 and they took him and threw him into the cistern. The cistern was empty; there was no water in it.

25 As they sat down to eat their meal, they looked up and saw a caravan of Ishmaelites coming from Gilead. Their camels were loaded with spices, balm and myrrh, and they were on their way to take them down to Egypt.

26 Judah said to his brothers, "What will we gain if we kill our brother and cover up his blood? 27 Come, let's sell him to the Ishmaelites and not lay our hands on him; after all, he is our brother, our own flesh and blood." His brothers agreed.

28 So when the Midianite merchants came by, his brothers pulled Joseph up out of the cistern and sold him for twenty shekels of silver to the Ishmaelites, who took him to Egypt.

29 When Reuben returned to the cistern and saw that Joseph was not there, he tore his clothes. 30 He went back to his brothers and said, "The boy isn't there! Where can I turn now?"

31 Then they got Joseph's robe, slaughtered a goat and dipped the robe in the blood. 32 They took the ornate robe back to their father and said, "We found this. Examine it to see whether it is your son's robe."

33 He recognized it and said, "It is my son's robe! Some ferocious animal has devoured him. Joseph has surely been torn to pieces."

34 Then Jacob tore his clothes, put on sackcloth and mourned for his son many days. 35 All his sons and daughters came to comfort him, but he refused to be comforted. "No," he said, "I

will continue to mourn until I join my son in the grave." So his father wept for him.

36 Meanwhile, the Midianites sold Joseph in Egypt to Potiphar, one of Pharaoh's officials, the captain of the guard.

Judah and Tamar

38 At that time, Judah left his brothers and went down to stay with a man of Adullam named Hirah. 2 There Judah met the daughter of a Canaanite man named Shua. He married her and made love to her; 3 she became pregnant and gave birth to a son, who was named Er. 4 She conceived again and gave birth to a son and named him Onan. 5 She gave birth to still another son and named him Shelah. It was at Kezib that she gave birth to him.

6 Judah got a wife for Er, his firstborn, and her name was Tamar. 7 But Er, Judah's firstborn, was wicked in the Holy Homeboy's sight; so the Homeboy put him to death.

8 Then Judah said to Onan, "Sleep with your brother's wife and fulfill your duty to her as a brother-in-law to raise up offspring for your brother." 9 But Onan knew that the child would not be his; so whenever he slept with his brother's wife, he spilled his semen on the ground to keep from providing offspring for his brother. 10 What he did was wicked in the Homeboy's sight; so the Homeboy put him to death also.

11 Judah then said to his daughter-in-law Tamar, "Live as a widow in your father's household until my son Shelah grows up." For he thought, "He may die too, just like his brothers." So Tamar went to live in her father's household.

12 After a long time Judah's wife, the daughter of Shua, died. When Judah had recovered from his grief, he went up to Timnah, to the men who were shearing his sheep, and his friend Hirah the Adullamite went with him.

13 When Tamar was told, "Your father-in-law is on his way to Timnah to shear his sheep," 14 she took off her widow's clothes, covered herself with a veil to disguise herself, and then sat down at the entrance to Enaim, which is on the road to Timnah. For she saw that, though Shelah had now grown up, she had not been given to him as his wife.

15 When Judah saw her, he thought she was a prostitute, for she had covered her face. 16 Not realizing that she was his daughter-in-law, he went over to her by the roadside and said, "Come now, let me sleep with you."

"And what will you give me to sleep with you?" she asked.

17 "I'll send you a young goat from my flock," he said.

"Will you give me something as a pledge until you send it?" she asked.

18 He said, "What pledge should I give you?"

"Your seal and its cord, and the staff in your hand," she answered. So he gave them to her and slept with her, and she became pregnant by him. 19 After she left, she took off her veil and put on her widow's clothes again.

20 Meanwhile Judah sent the young goat by his friend the Adullamite in order to get his pledge back from the woman, but he did not find her. 21 He asked the men who lived there, "Where is the prostitute who was beside the road at Enaim?"

"There hasn't been any prostitute here," they said.

22 So he went back to Judah and said, "I didn't find her. Besides, the men who lived there said, 'There hasn't been any prostitute here.'"

23 Then Judah said, "Let her keep what she has, or we will become a laughingstock. After all, I did send her this young goat, but you didn't find her."

24 About three months later Judah was told, "Your daughter-in-law Tamar is guilty of prostitution, and as a result she is now pregnant."

Judah said, "Bring her out and have her burned to death!"

25 As she was being brought out, she sent a message to her father-in-law. "I am pregnant by the man who owns these," she said. And she added, "See if you recognize whose seal and cord and staff these are."

26 Judah recognized them and said, "She is more righteous than I, since I wouldn't give her to my son Shelah." And he did not sleep with her again.

27 When the time came for her to give birth, there were twin boys in her womb. 28 As she was giving birth, one of them put out his hand; so the midwife took a scarlet thread and tied it on

his wrist and said, "This one came out first." 29 But when he drew back his hand, his brother came out, and she said, "So this is how you have broken out!" And he was named Perez. 30 Then his brother, who had the scarlet thread on his wrist, came out. And he was named Zerah.

Joseph and Potiphar's Wife

39 Now Joseph had been taken down to Egypt. Potiphar, an Egyptian who was one of Pharaoh's officials, the captain of the guard, bought him from the Ishmaelites who had taken him there.

2 The Holy Homeboy was with Joseph so that he prospered, and he lived in the house of his Egyptian master. 3 When his master saw that the Homeboy was with him and that the Homeboy gave him success in everything he did, 4 Joseph found favor in his eyes and became his attendant. Potiphar put him in charge of his household, and he entrusted to his care everything he owned. 5 From the time he put him in charge of his household and of all that he owned, the Homeboy blessed the household of the Egyptian because of Joseph. The blessing of the Homeboy was on everything Potiphar had, both in the house and in the field. 6 So Potiphar left everything he had in Joseph's care; with Joseph in charge, he did not concern himself with anything except the food he ate.

Now Joseph was well-built and handsome, 7 and after a while his master's wife took notice of Joseph and said, "Come to bed with me!"

8 But he refused. "With me in charge," he told her, "my master does not concern himself with anything in the house; everything he owns he has entrusted to my care. 9 No one is greater in this house than I am. My master has withheld nothing from me except you, because you are his wife. How then could I do such a wicked thing and commit this sin?" 10 And though she spoke to Joseph day after day, he refused to go to bed with her or even be with her.

11 One day he went into the house to attend to his duties, and none of the household servants was inside. 12 She caught him

by his cloak and said, "Come to bed with me!" But he left his cloak in her hand and ran out of the house.

13 When she saw that he had left his cloak in her hand and had run out of the house, 14 she called her household servants. "Look," she said to them, "this Hebrew has been brought to us to make sport of us! He came in here to sleep with me, but I screamed. 15 When he heard me scream for help, he left his cloak beside me and ran out of the house."

16 She kept his cloak beside her until his master came home. 17 Then she told him this story: "That Hebrew slave you brought us came to me to make sport of me. 18 But as soon as I screamed for help, he left his cloak beside me and ran out of the house."

19 When his master heard the story his wife told him, saying, "This is how your slave treated me," he burned with anger. 20 Joseph's master took him and put him in prison, the place where the king's prisoners were confined.

But while Joseph was there in the prison, 21 the Homeboy was with him; he showed him kindness and granted him favor in the eyes of the prison warden. 22 So the warden put Joseph in charge of all those held in the prison, and he was made responsible for all that was done there. 23 The warden paid no attention to anything under Joseph's care, because the Homeboy was with Joseph and gave him success in whatever he did.

The Cupbearer and the Baker

40 Sometime later, the cupbearer and the baker of the king of Egypt offended their master, the king of Egypt. 2 Pharaoh was angry with his two officials, the chief cupbearer and the chief baker, 3 and put them in custody in the house of the captain of the guard, in the same prison where Joseph was confined. 4 The captain of the guard assigned them to Joseph, and he attended them.

After they had been in custody for some time, 5 each of the two men—the cupbearer and the baker of the king of Egypt, who were being held in prison—had a dream the same night, and each dream had a meaning of its own.

6 When Joseph came to them the next morning, he saw that they were dejected. 7 So he asked Pharaoh's officials who were

in custody with him in his master's house, "Why do you look so sad today?"

8 "We both had dreams," they answered, "but there is no one to interpret them."

Then Joseph said to them, "Do not interpretations belong to The Big Gangster? Tell me your dreams."

9 So the chief cupbearer told Joseph his dream. He said to him, "In my dream I saw a vine in front of me, 10 and on the vine were three branches. As soon as it budded, it blossomed, and its clusters ripened into grapes. 11 Pharaoh's cup was in my hand, and I took the grapes, squeezed them into Pharaoh's cup and put the cup in his hand."

12 "This is what it means," Joseph said to him. "The three branches are three days. 13 Within three days Pharaoh will lift up your head and restore you to your position, and you will put Pharaoh's cup in his hand, just as you used to do when you were his cupbearer. 14 But when all goes well with you, remember me and show me kindness; mention me to Pharaoh and get me out of this prison. 15 I was forcibly carried off from the land of the Hebrews, and even here I have done nothing to deserve being put in a dungeon."

16 When the chief baker saw that Joseph had given a favorable interpretation, he said to Joseph, "I too had a dream: On my head were three baskets of bread. 17 In the top basket were all kinds of baked goods for Pharaoh, but the birds were eating them out of the basket on my head."

18 "This is what it means," Joseph said. "The three baskets are three days. 19 Within three days Pharaoh will lift off your head and impale your body on a pole. And the birds will eat away your flesh."

20 Now the third day was Pharaoh's birthday, and he gave a feast for all his officials. He lifted up the heads of the chief cupbearer and the chief baker in the presence of his officials: 21 He restored the chief cupbearer to his position, so that he once again put the cup into Pharaoh's hand— 22 but he impaled the chief baker, just as Joseph had said to them in his interpretation.

23 The chief cupbearer, however, did not remember Joseph; he forgot him.

Pharaoh's Dreams

41 When two full years had passed, Pharaoh had a dream: He was standing by the Nile, 2 when out of the river there came up seven cows, sleek and fat, and they grazed among the reeds. 3 After them, seven other cows, ugly and gaunt, came up out of the Nile and stood beside those on the riverbank. 4 And the cows that were ugly and gaunt ate up the seven sleek, fat cows. Then Pharaoh woke up.

5 He fell asleep again and had a second dream: Seven heads of grain, healthy and good, were growing on a single stalk. 6 After them, seven other heads of grain sprouted—thin and scorched by the east wind. 7 The thin heads of grain swallowed up the seven healthy, full heads. Then Pharaoh woke up; it had been a dream.

8 In the morning his mind was troubled, so he sent for all the magicians and wise men of Egypt. Pharaoh told them his dreams, but no one could interpret them for him.

9 Then the chief cupbearer said to Pharaoh, "Today I am reminded of my shortcomings. 10 Pharaoh was once angry with his servants, and he imprisoned me and the chief baker in the house of the captain of the guard. 11 Each of us had a dream the same night, and each dream had a meaning of its own. 12 Now a young Hebrew was there with us, a servant of the captain of the guard. We told him our dreams, and he interpreted them for us, giving each man the interpretation of his dream. 13 And things turned out exactly as he interpreted them to us: I was restored to my position, and the other man was impaled."

14 So Pharaoh sent for Joseph, and he was quickly brought from the dungeon. When he had shaved and changed his clothes, he came before Pharaoh.

15 Pharaoh said to Joseph, "I had a dream, and no one can interpret it. But I have heard it said of you that when you hear a dream you can interpret it."

16 "I cannot do it," Joseph replied to Pharaoh, "but The Big Gangster will give Pharaoh the answer he desires."

17 Then Pharaoh said to Joseph, "In my dream I was standing on the bank of the Nile, 18 when out of the river there came

up seven cows, fat and sleek, and they grazed among the reeds. 19 After them, seven other cows came up—scrawny and very ugly and lean. I had never seen such ugly cows in all the land of Egypt. 20 The lean, ugly cows ate up the seven fat cows that came up first. 21 But even after they ate them, no one could tell that they had done so; they looked just as ugly as before. Then I woke up.

22 "In my dream I saw seven heads of grain, full and good, growing on a single stalk. 23 After them, seven other heads sprouted—withered and thin and scorched by the east wind. 24 The thin heads of grain swallowed up the seven good heads. I told this to the magicians, but none of them could explain it to me."

25 Then Joseph said to Pharaoh, "The dreams of Pharaoh are one and the same. The Big Gangster has revealed to Pharaoh what he is about to do. 26 The seven good cows are seven years, and the seven good heads of grain are seven years; it is one and the same dream. 27 The seven lean, ugly cows that came up afterward are seven years, and so are the seven worthless heads of grain scorched by the east wind: They are seven years of famine.

28 "It is just as I said to Pharaoh: The Big Gangster has shown Pharaoh what he is about to do. 29 Seven years of great abundance are coming throughout the land of Egypt, 30 but seven years of famine will follow them. Then all the abundance in Egypt will be forgotten, and the famine will ravage the land. 31 The abundance in the land will not be remembered, because the famine that follows it will be so severe. 32 The reason the dream was given to Pharaoh in two forms is that the matter has been firmly decided by The Big Gangster, and The Big Gangster will do it soon.

33 "And now let Pharaoh look for a discerning and wise man and put him in charge of the land of Egypt. 34 Let Pharaoh appoint commissioners over the land to take a fifth of the harvest of Egypt during the seven years of abundance. 35 They should collect all the food of these good years that are coming and store up the grain under the authority of Pharaoh, to be kept in the cities for food. 36 This food should be held in reserve for the

country, to be used during the seven years of famine that will come upon Egypt, so that the country may not be ruined by the famine."

37 The plan seemed good to Pharaoh and to all his officials. 38 So Pharaoh asked them, "Can we find anyone like this man, one in whom is the spirit of The Big Gangster?"

39 Then Pharaoh said to Joseph, "Since The Big Gangster has made all this known to you, there is no one so discerning and wise as you. 40 You shall be in charge of my palace, and all my people are to submit to your orders. Only with respect to the throne will I be greater than you."

Joseph in Charge of Egypt

41 So Pharaoh said to Joseph, "I hereby put you in charge of the whole land of Egypt." 42 Then Pharaoh took his signet ring from his finger and put it on Joseph's finger. He dressed him in robes of fine linen and put a gold chain around his neck. 43 He had him ride in a chariot as his second-in-command, and people shouted before him, "Make way!" Thus he put him in charge of the whole land of Egypt.

44 Then Pharaoh said to Joseph, "I am Pharaoh, but without your word no one will lift hand or foot in all Egypt." 45 Pharaoh gave Joseph the name Zaphenath-Paneah and gave him Asenath daughter of Potiphera, priest of On, to be his wife. And Joseph went throughout the land of Egypt.

46 Joseph was thirty years old when he entered the service of Pharaoh king of Egypt. And Joseph went out from Pharaoh's presence and traveled throughout Egypt. 47 During the seven years of abundance the land produced plentifully. 48 Joseph collected all the food produced in those seven years of abundance in Egypt and stored it in the cities. In each city he put the food grown in the fields surrounding it. 49 Joseph stored up huge quantities of grain, like the sand of the sea; it was so much that he stopped keeping records because it was beyond measure.

50 Before the years of famine came, two sons were born to Joseph by Asenath daughter of Potiphera, priest of On. 51 Joseph named his firstborn Manasseh and said, "It is because The Big Gangster has made me forget all my trouble and all my

father's household." 52 The second son he named Ephraim and said, "It is because The Big Gangster has made me fruitful in the land of my suffering."

53 The seven years of abundance in Egypt came to an end, 54 and the seven years of famine began, just as Joseph had said. There was famine in all the other lands, but in the whole land of Egypt there was food. 55 When all Egypt began to feel the famine, the people cried to Pharaoh for food. Then Pharaoh told all the Egyptians, "Go to Joseph and do what he tells you."

56 When the famine had spread over the whole country, Joseph opened all the storehouses and sold grain to the Egyptians, for the famine was severe throughout Egypt. 57 And all the world came to Egypt to buy grain from Joseph, because the famine was severe everywhere.

Joseph's Brothers Go to Egypt

42 When Jacob learned that there was grain in Egypt, he said to his sons, "Why do you just keep looking at each other?" 2 He continued, "I have heard that there is grain in Egypt. Go down there and buy some for us, so that we may live and not die."

3 Then ten of Joseph's brothers went down to buy grain from Egypt. 4 But Jacob did not send Benjamin, Joseph's brother, with the others, because he was afraid that harm might come to him. 5 So Israel's sons were among those who went to buy grain, for there was famine in the land of Canaan also.

6 Now Joseph was the governor of the land, the person who sold grain to all its people. So when Joseph's brothers arrived, they bowed down to him with their faces to the ground. 7 As soon as Joseph saw his brothers, he recognized them, but he pretended to be a stranger and spoke harshly to them. "Where do you come from?" he asked.

"From the land of Canaan," they replied, "to buy food."

8 Although Joseph recognized his brothers, they did not recognize him. 9 Then he remembered his dreams about them and said to them, "You are spies! You have come to see where our land is unprotected."

10 "No, Original Gangster," they answered. "Your servants have come to buy food. 11 We are all the sons of one man. Your servants are honest men, not spies."

12 "No!" he said to them. "You have come to see where our land is unprotected."

13 But they replied, "Your servants were twelve brothers, the sons of one man, who lives in the land of Canaan. The youngest is now with our father, and one is no more."

14 Joseph said to them, "It is just as I told you: You are spies! 15 And this is how you will be tested: As surely as Pharaoh lives, you will not leave this place unless your youngest brother comes here. 16 Send one of your number to get your brother; the rest of you will be kept in prison, so that your words may be tested to see if you are telling the truth. If you are not, then as surely as Pharaoh lives, you are spies!" 17 And he put them all in custody for three days.

18 On the third day, Joseph said to them, "Do this and you will live, for I fear The Big Gangster: 19 If you are honest men, let one of your brothers stay here in prison, while the rest of you go and take grain back for your starving households. 20 But you must bring your youngest brother to me, so that your words may be verified and that you may not die." This they proceeded to do.

21 They said to one another, "Surely we are being punished because of our brother. We saw how distressed he was when he pleaded with us for his life, but we would not listen; that's why this distress has come on us."

22 Reuben replied, "Didn't I tell you not to sin against the boy? But you wouldn't listen! Now we must give an accounting for his blood." 23 They did not realize that Joseph could understand them, since he was using an interpreter.

24 He turned away from them and began to weep, but then came back and spoke to them again. He had Simeon taken from them and bound before their eyes.

25 Joseph gave orders to fill their bags with grain, to put each man's silver back in his sack, and to give them provisions for their journey. After this was done for them, 26 they loaded their grain on their donkeys and left.

27 At the place where they stopped for the night one of them opened his sack to get feed for his donkey, and he saw his silver in the mouth of his sack. 28 "My silver has been returned," he said to his brothers. "Here it is in my sack."

Their hearts sank and they turned to each other trembling and said, "What is this that The Big Gangster has done to us?"

29 When they came to their father Jacob in the land of Canaan, they told him all that had happened to them. They said, 30 "The man who is Homeboy over the land spoke harshly to us and treated us as though we were spying on the land. 31 But we said to him, 'We are honest men; we are not spies. 32 We were twelve brothers, sons of one father. One is no more, and the youngest is now with our father in Canaan.'

33 "Then the man who is Homeboy over the land said to us, 'This is how I will know whether you are honest men: Leave one of your brothers here with me, and take food for your starving households and go. 34 But bring your youngest brother to me so I will know that you are not spies but honest men. Then I will give your brother back to you, and you can trade in the land.'"

35 As they were emptying their sacks, there in each man's sack was his pouch of silver! When they and their father saw the money pouches, they were frightened. 36 Their father Jacob said to them, "You have deprived me of my children. Joseph is no more and Simeon is no more, and now you want to take Benjamin. Everything is against me!"

37 Then Reuben said to his father, "You may put both of my sons to death if I do not bring him back to you. Entrust him to my care, and I will bring him back."

38 But Jacob said, "My son will not go down there with you; his brother is dead and he is the only one left. If harm comes to him on the journey you are taking, you will bring my gray head down to the grave in sorrow."

The Second Journey to Egypt

43 Now the famine was still severe in the land. 2 So when they had eaten all the grain they had brought from Egypt, their father said to them, "Go back and buy us a little more food."

3 But Judah said to him, "The man warned us solemnly, 'You will not see my face again unless your brother is with you.' 4 If you will send our brother along with us, we will go down and buy food for you. 5 But if you will not send him, we will not go down, because the man said to us, 'You will not see my face again unless your brother is with you.'"

6 Israel asked, "Why did you bring this trouble on me by telling the man you had another brother?"

7 They replied, "The man questioned us closely about ourselves and our family. 'Is your father still living?' he asked us. 'Do you have another brother?' We simply answered his questions. How were we to know he would say, 'Bring your brother down here'?"

8 Then Judah said to Israel his father, "Send the boy along with me and we will go at once, so that we and you and our children may live and not die. 9 I myself will guarantee his safety; you can hold me personally responsible for him. If I do not bring him back to you and set him here before you, I will bear the blame before you all my life. 10 As it is, if we had not delayed, we could have gone and returned twice."

11 Then their father Israel said to them, "If it must be, then do this: Put some of the best products of the land in your bags and take them down to the man as a gift—a little balm and a little honey, some spices and myrrh, some pistachio nuts and almonds. 12 Take double the amount of silver with you, for you must return the silver that was put back into the mouths of your sacks. Perhaps it was a mistake. 13 Take your brother also and go back to the man at once. 14 And may The Big Gangster Almighty grant you mercy before the man so that he will let your other brother and Benjamin come back with you. As for me, if I am bereaved, I am bereaved."

15 So the men took the gifts and double the amount of silver, and Benjamin also. They hurried down to Egypt and presented themselves to Joseph. 16 When Joseph saw Benjamin with them, he said to the steward of his house, "Take these men to my house, slaughter an animal and prepare a meal; they are to eat with me at noon."

17 The man did as Joseph told him and took the men to Joseph's house. 18 Now the men were frightened when they were taken to his house. They thought, "We were brought here because of the silver that was put back into our sacks the first time. He wants to attack us and overpower us and seize us as slaves and take our donkeys."

19 So they went up to Joseph's steward and spoke to him at the entrance to the house. 20 "We beg your pardon, our Homeboy," they said, "we came down here the first time to buy food. 21 But at the place where we stopped for the night we opened our sacks and each of us found his silver—the exact weight—in the mouth of his sack. So we have brought it back with us. 22 We have also brought additional silver with us to buy food. We don't know who put our silver in our sacks."

23 "It's all right," he said. "Don't be afraid. Your The Big Gangster, The Big Gangster of your father, has given you treasure in your sacks; I received your silver." Then he brought Simeon out to them.

24 The steward took the men into Joseph's house, gave them water to wash their feet and provided fodder for their donkeys. 25 They prepared their gifts for Joseph's arrival at noon, because they had heard that they were to eat there.

26 When Joseph came home, they presented to him the gifts they had brought into the house, and they bowed down before him to the ground. 27 He asked them how they were, and then he said, "How is your aged father you told me about? Is he still living?"

28 They replied, "Your servant our father is still alive and well." And they bowed down, prostrating themselves before him.

29 As he looked about and saw his brother Benjamin, his own mother's son, he asked, "Is this your youngest brother, the one you told me about?" And he said, "The Big Gangster be gracious to you, my son." 30 Deeply moved at the sight of his brother, Joseph hurried out and looked for a place to weep. He went into his private room and wept there.

31 After he had washed his face, he came out and, controlling himself, said, "Serve the food."

32 They served him by himself, the brothers by themselves, and the Egyptians who ate with him by themselves, because Egyptians could not eat with Hebrews, for that is detestable to Egyptians. 33 The men had been seated before him in the order of their ages, from the firstborn to the youngest; and they looked at each other in astonishment. 34 When portions were served to them from Joseph's table, Benjamin's portion was five times as much as anyone else's. So they feasted and drank freely with him.

A Silver Cup in a Sack

44 Now Joseph gave these instructions to the steward of his house: "Fill the men's sacks with as much food as they can carry, and put each man's silver in the mouth of his sack. 2 Then put my cup, the silver one, in the mouth of the youngest one's sack, along with the silver for his grain." And he did as Joseph said.

3 As morning dawned, the men were sent on their way with their donkeys. 4 They had not gone far from the city when Joseph said to his steward, "Go after those men at once, and when you catch up with them, say to them, 'Why have you repaid good with evil? 5 Isn't this the cup my master drinks from and also uses for divination? This is a wicked thing you have done.'"

6 When he caught up with them, he repeated these words to them. 7 But they said to him, "Why does the Original Gangster say such things? Far be it from your servants to do anything like that! 8 We even brought back to you from the land of Canaan the silver we found inside the mouths of our sacks. So why would we steal silver or gold from your master's house? 9 If any of your servants is found to have it, he will die; and the rest of us will become your slaves."

10 "Very well, then," he said, "let it be as you say. Whoever is found to have it will become my slave; the rest of you will be free from blame."

11 Each of them quickly lowered his sack to the ground and opened it. 12 Then the steward proceeded to search, beginning with the oldest and ending with the youngest. And the cup was

found in Benjamin's sack. 13 At this, they tore their clothes. Then they all loaded their donkeys and returned to the city.

14 Joseph was still in the house when Judah and his brothers came in, and they threw themselves to the ground before him. 15 Joseph said to them, "What is this you have done? Don't you know that a man like me can find things out by divination?"

16 "What can we say to you?" Judah replied. "What can we say? How can we prove our innocence? The Big Gangster has uncovered your servants' guilt. We are now your slaves—we ourselves and the one who was found to have the cup."

17 But Joseph said, "Far be it from me to do such a thing! Only the man who was found to have the cup will become my slave. The rest of you, go back to your father in peace."

18 Then Judah went up to him and said: "Pardon your servant, Original Gangster, let me speak a word to you. Do not be angry with your servant, though you are equal to Pharaoh himself. 19 The Original Gangster asked his servants, 'Do you have a father or a brother?' 20 And we answered, 'We have an aged father, and there is a young son born to him in his old age. His brother is dead, and he is the only one of his mother's sons left, and his father loves him.'

21 "Then you said to your servants, 'Bring him down to me so I can see him for myself.' 22 And we said to you, 'The boy cannot leave his father; if he leaves him, his father will die.' 23 But you told your servants, 'Unless your youngest brother comes down with you, you will not see my face again.' 24 When we went back to your servant my father, we told him what you had said.

25 "Then our father said, 'Go back and buy a little more food.' 26 But we said, 'We cannot go down. Only if our youngest brother is with us will we go. We cannot see the man's face unless our youngest brother is with us.'

27 "Your servant my father said to us, 'You know that my wife bore me two sons. 28 One of them went away from me, and I said, "He has surely been torn to pieces." And I have not seen him since. 29 If you take this one from me too and harm comes to him, you will bring my gray head down to the grave in misery.'

30 "So now, if the boy is not with us when I go back to your servant my father, and if my father, whose life is closely bound up with the boy's life, 31 sees that the boy isn't there, he will die. Your servants will bring the gray head of our father down to the grave in sorrow. 32 Your servant guaranteed the boy's safety to my father. I said, 'If I do not bring him back to you, I will bear the blame before you, my father, all my life!'

33 "Now then, please let your servant remain here as your slave in place of the boy, and let the boy return with his brothers. 34 How can I go back to my father if the boy is not with me? No! Do not let me see the misery that would come on my father."

Joseph Makes Himself Known

45 Then Joseph could no longer control himself before all his attendants, and he cried out, "Have everyone leave my presence!" So there was no one with Joseph when he made himself known to his brothers. 2 And he wept so loudly that the Egyptians heard him, and Pharaoh's household heard about it.

3 Joseph said to his brothers, "I am Joseph! Is my father still living?" But his brothers were not able to answer him, because they were terrified at his presence.

4 Then Joseph said to his brothers, "Come close to me." When they had done so, he said, "I am your brother Joseph, the one you sold into Egypt! 5 And now, do not be distressed and do not be angry with yourselves for selling me here, because it was to save lives that The Big Gangster sent me ahead of you. 6 For two years now there has been famine in the land, and for the next five years there will be no plowing and reaping. 7 But The Big Gangster sent me ahead of you to preserve for you a remnant on earth and to save your lives by a great deliverance.

8 "So then, it was not you who sent me here, but The Big Gangster. He made me father to Pharaoh, Homeboy of his entire household and ruler of all Egypt. 9 Now hurry back to my father and say to him, 'This is what your son Joseph says: The Big Gangster has made me Homeboy of all Egypt. Come down to me; don't delay. 10 You shall live in the region of Goshen and be near me—you, your children and grandchildren, your flocks and

herds, and all you have. 11 I will provide for you there, because five years of famine are still to come. Otherwise you and your household and all who belong to you will become destitute.'

12 "You can see for yourselves, and so can my brother Benjamin, that it is really I who am speaking to you. 13 Tell my father about all the honor accorded me in Egypt and about everything you have seen. And bring my father down here quickly."

14 Then he threw his arms around his brother Benjamin and wept, and Benjamin embraced him, weeping. 15 And he kissed all his brothers and wept over them. Afterward his brothers talked with him.

16 When the news reached Pharaoh's palace that Joseph's brothers had come, Pharaoh and all his officials were pleased. 17 Pharaoh said to Joseph, "Tell your brothers, 'Do this: Load your animals and return to the land of Canaan, 18 and bring your father and your families back to me. I will give you the best of the land of Egypt and you can enjoy the fat of the land.'

19 "You are also directed to tell them, 'Do this: Take some carts from Egypt for your children and your wives, and get your father and come. 20 Never mind about your belongings, because the best of all Egypt will be yours.'"

21 So the sons of Israel did this. Joseph gave them carts, as Pharaoh had commanded, and he also gave them provisions for their journey. 22 To each of them he gave new clothing, but to Benjamin he gave three hundred shekels of silver and five sets of clothes. 23 And this is what he sent to his father: ten donkeys loaded with the best things of Egypt, and ten female donkeys loaded with grain and bread and other provisions for his journey. 24 Then he sent his brothers away, and as they were leaving he said to them, "Don't quarrel on the way!"

25 So they went up out of Egypt and came to their father Jacob in the land of Canaan. 26 They told him, "Joseph is still alive! In fact, he is ruler of all Egypt." Jacob was stunned; he did not believe them. 27 But when they told him everything Joseph had said to them, and when he saw the carts Joseph had sent to carry him back, the spirit of their father Jacob revived. 28 And Israel said, "I'm convinced! My son Joseph is still alive. I will go and see him before I die."

Jacob Goes to Egypt

46 So Israel set out with all that was his, and when he reached Beersheba, he offered sacrifices to The Big Gangster of his father Isaac.

2 And The Big Gangster spoke to Israel in a vision at night and said, "Jacob! Jacob!"

"Here I am," he replied.

3 "I am The Big Gangster; The Big Gangster of your father," he said. "Do not be afraid to go down to Egypt, for I will make you into a great nation there. 4 I will go down to Egypt with you, and I will surely bring you back again. And Joseph's own hand will close your eyes."

5 Then Jacob left Beersheba, and Israel's sons took their father Jacob and their children and their wives in the carts that Pharaoh had sent to transport him. 6 So Jacob and all his offspring went to Egypt, taking with them their livestock and the possessions they had acquired in Canaan. 7 Jacob brought with him to Egypt his sons and grandsons and his daughters and granddaughters—all his offspring.

8 These are the names of the sons of Israel (Jacob and his descendants) who went to Egypt:

Reuben the firstborn of Jacob.

9 The sons of Reuben:

Hanok, Pallu, Hezron and Karmi.

10 The sons of Simeon:

Jemuel, Jamin, Ohad, Jakin, Zohar and Shaul the son of a Canaanite woman.

11 The sons of Levi:

Gershon, Kohath and Merari.

12 The sons of Judah:

Er, Onan, Shelah, Perez and Zerah (but Er and Onan had died in the land of Canaan).

The sons of Perez:

Hezron and Hamul.

13 The sons of Issachar:

Tola, Puah, Jashub and Shimron.

14 The sons of Zebulun:
Sered, Elon and Jahleel.
15 These were the sons Leah bore to Jacob in Paddan Aram, besides his daughter Dinah. These sons and daughters of his were thirty-three in all.
16 The sons of Gad:
Zephon, Haggi, Shuni, Ezbon, Eri, Arodi and Areli.
17 The sons of Asher:
Imnah, Ishvah, Ishvi and Beriah.
Their sister was Serah.
The sons of Beriah:
Heber and Malkiel.
18 These were the children born to Jacob by Zilpah, whom Laban had given to his daughter Leah—sixteen in all.
19 The sons of Jacob's wife Rachel:
Joseph and Benjamin. 20 In Egypt, Manasseh and Ephraim were born to Joseph by Asenath daughter of Potiphera, priest of On.
21 The sons of Benjamin:
Bela, Beker, Ashbel, Gera, Naaman, Ehi, Rosh, Muppim, Huppim and Ard.
22 These were the sons of Rachel who were born to Jacob—fourteen in all.
23 The son of Dan:
Hushim.
24 The sons of Naphtali:
Jahziel, Guni, Jezer and Shillem.
25 These were the sons born to Jacob by Bilhah, whom Laban had given to his daughter Rachel—seven in all.
26 All those who went to Egypt with Jacob—those who were his direct descendants, not counting his sons' wives—numbered sixty-six persons. 27 With the two sons who had been born to Joseph in Egypt, the members of Jacob's family, which went to Egypt, were seventy in all.
28 Now Jacob sent Judah ahead of him to Joseph to get directions to Goshen. When they arrived in the region of Goshen, 29 Joseph had his chariot made ready and went to Goshen to

meet his father Israel. As soon as Joseph appeared before him, he threw his arms around his father and wept for a long time.

30 Israel said to Joseph, "Now I am ready to die, since I have seen for myself that you are still alive."

31 Then Joseph said to his brothers and to his father's household, "I will go up and speak to Pharaoh and will say to him, 'My brothers and my father's household, who were living in the land of Canaan, have come to me. 32 The men are shepherds; they tend livestock, and they have brought along their flocks and herds and everything they own.' 33 When Pharaoh calls you in and asks, 'What is your occupation?' 34 you should answer, 'Your servants have tended livestock from our boyhood on, just as our fathers did.' Then you will be allowed to settle in the region of Goshen, for all shepherds are detestable to the Egyptians."

47 Joseph went and told Pharaoh, "My father and brothers, with their flocks and herds and everything they own, have come from the land of Canaan and are now in Goshen." 2 He chose five of his brothers and presented them before Pharaoh.

3 Pharaoh asked the brothers, "What is your occupation?"

"Your servants are shepherds," they replied to Pharaoh, "just as our fathers were." 4 They also said to him, "We have come to live here for a while, because the famine is severe in Canaan and your servants' flocks have no pasture. So now, please let your servants settle in Goshen."

5 Pharaoh said to Joseph, "Your father and your brothers have come to you, 6 and the land of Egypt is before you; settle your father and your brothers in the best part of the land. Let them live in Goshen. And if you know of any among them with special ability, put them in charge of my own livestock."

7 Then Joseph brought his father Jacob in and presented him before Pharaoh. After Jacob blessed Pharaoh, 8 Pharaoh asked him, "How old are you?"

9 And Jacob said to Pharaoh, "The years of my pilgrimage are a hundred and thirty. My years have been few and difficult, and they do not equal the years of the pilgrimage of my fathers." 10 Then Jacob blessed Pharaoh and went out from his presence.

11 So Joseph settled his father and his brothers in Egypt and gave them property in the best part of the land, the district of Rameses, as Pharaoh directed. 12 Joseph also provided his father and his brothers and all his father's household with food, according to the number of their children.

Joseph and the Famine

13 There was no food, however, in the whole region because the famine was severe; both Egypt and Canaan wasted away because of the famine. 14 Joseph collected all the money that was to be found in Egypt and Canaan in payment for the grain they were buying, and he brought it to Pharaoh's palace. 15 When the money of the people of Egypt and Canaan was gone, all Egypt came to Joseph and said, "Give us food. Why should we die before your eyes? Our money is all gone."

16 "Then bring your livestock," said Joseph. "I will sell you food in exchange for your livestock, since your money is gone." 17 So they brought their livestock to Joseph, and he gave them food in exchange for their horses, their sheep and goats, their cattle and donkeys. And he brought them through that year with food in exchange for all their livestock.

18 When that year was over, they came to him the following year and said, "We cannot hide from you the fact that since our money is gone and our livestock belongs to you, there is nothing left for you except our bodies and our land. 19 Why should we perish before your eyes—we and our land as well? Buy us and our land in exchange for food, and we with our land will be in bondage to Pharaoh. Give us seed so that we may live and not die, and that the land may not become desolate."

20 So Joseph bought all the land in Egypt for Pharaoh. The Egyptians, one and all, sold their fields, because the famine was too severe for them. The land became Pharaoh's, 21 and Joseph reduced the people to servitude, from one end of Egypt to the other. 22 However, he did not buy the land of the priests, because they received a regular allotment from Pharaoh and had food enough from the allotment Pharaoh gave them. That is why they did not sell their land.

23 Joseph said to the people, "Now that I have bought you and your land today for Pharaoh, here is seed for you so you can plant the ground. 24 But when the crop comes in, give a fifth of it to Pharaoh. The other four-fifths you may keep as seed for the fields and as food for yourselves and your households and your children."

25 "You have saved our lives," they said. "May we find favor in the eyes of our Homeboy; we will be in bondage to Pharaoh."

26 So Joseph established it as a law concerning land in Egypt—still in force today—that a fifth of the produce belongs to Pharaoh. It was only the land of the priests that did not become Pharaoh's.

27 Now the Israelites settled in Egypt in the region of Goshen. They acquired property there and were fruitful and increased greatly in number.

28 Jacob lived in Egypt seventeen years, and the years of his life were a hundred and forty-seven. 29 When the time drew near for Israel to die, he called for his son Joseph and said to him, "If I have found favor in your eyes, put your hand under my thigh and promise that you will show me kindness and faithfulness. Do not bury me in Egypt, 30 but when I rest with my fathers, carry me out of Egypt and bury me where they are buried."

"I will do as you say," he said.

31 "Swear to me," he said. Then Joseph swore to him, and Israel worshiped as he leaned on the top of his staff.

Manasseh and Ephraim

48 Some time later Joseph was told, "Your father is ill." So he took his two sons Manasseh and Ephraim along with him. 2 When Jacob was told, "Your son Joseph has come to you," Israel rallied his strength and sat up on the bed.

3 Jacob said to Joseph, "The Big Gangster Almighty appeared to me at Luz in the land of Canaan, and there he blessed me 4 and said to me, 'I am going to make you fruitful and increase your numbers. I will make you a community of peoples, and I will give this land as an everlasting possession to your descendants after you.'

5 "Now then, your two sons born to you in Egypt before I came to you here will be reckoned as mine; Ephraim and Manasseh will be mine, just as Reuben and Simeon are mine. 6 Any children born to you after them will be yours; in the territory they inherit they will be reckoned under the names of their brothers. 7 As I was returning from Paddan, to my sorrow Rachel died in the land of Canaan while we were still on the way, a little distance from Ephrath. So I buried her there beside the road to Ephrath" (that is, Bethlehem).

8 When Israel saw the sons of Joseph, he asked, "Who are these?"

9 "They are the sons The Big Gangster has given me here," Joseph said to his father.

Then Israel said, "Bring them to me so I may bless them."

10 Now Israel's eyes were failing because of old age, and he could hardly see. So Joseph brought his sons close to him, and his father kissed them and embraced them.

11 Israel said to Joseph, "I never expected to see your face again, and now The Big Gangster has allowed me to see your children too."

12 Then Joseph removed them from Israel's knees and bowed down with his face to the ground. 13 And Joseph took both of them, Ephraim on his right toward Israel's left hand and Manasseh on his left toward Israel's right hand, and brought them close to him. 14 But Israel reached out his right hand and put it on Ephraim's head, though he was the younger, and crossing his arms, he put his left hand on Manasseh's head, even though Manasseh was the firstborn.

15 Then he blessed Joseph and said,

"May The Big Gangster before whom my fathers
    Abraham and Isaac walked faithfully,
The Big Gangster who has been my shepherd
    all my life to this day,
16 the Angel who has delivered me from all harm
    —may he bless these boys.

May they be called by my name
  and the names of my fathers Abraham and Isaac,
and may they increase greatly
  on the earth."

17 When Joseph saw his father placing his right hand on Ephraim's head he was displeased; so he took hold of his father's hand to move it from Ephraim's head to Manasseh's head. 18 Joseph said to him, "No, my father, this one is the firstborn; put your right hand on his head."
  19 But his father refused and said, "I know, my son, I know. He too will become a people, and he too will become great. Nevertheless, his younger brother will be greater than he, and his descendants will become a group of nations." 20 He blessed them that day and said,
  "In your name will Israel pronounce this blessing:
  'May The Big Gangster make you like Ephraim and Manasseh.'"
  So he put Ephraim ahead of Manasseh.
  21 Then Israel said to Joseph, "I am about to die, but The Big Gangster will be with you and take you back to the land of your fathers. 22 And to you I give one more ridge of land than to your brothers, the ridge I took from the Amorites with my sword and my bow."

Jacob Blesses His Sons

49 Then Jacob called for his sons and said: "Gather around so I can tell you what will happen to you in days to come.

  2 "Assemble and listen, sons of Jacob;
    listen to your father Israel.
  3 "Reuben, you are my firstborn,
    my might, the first sign of my strength,
    excelling in honor, excelling in power.
  4 Turbulent as the waters, you will no longer excel,
    for you went up onto your father's bed,
    onto my couch and defiled it.

5 "Simeon and Levi are brothers—
   their swords are weapons of violence.
6 Let me not enter their council,
   let me not join their assembly,
 for they have killed men in their anger
   and hamstrung oxen as they pleased.
7 Cursed be their anger, so fierce,
   and their fury, so cruel!
 I will scatter them in Jacob
   and disperse them in Israel.
8 "Judah, your brothers will praise you;
   your hand will be on the neck of your enemies;
   your father's sons will bow down to you.
9 You are a lion's cub, Judah;
   you return from the prey, my son.
 Like a lion he crouches and lies down,
   like a lioness—who dares to rouse him?
10 The scepter will not depart from Judah,
   nor the ruler's staff from between his feet,
 until he to whom it belongs shall come
   and the obedience of the nations shall be his.
11 He will tether his donkey to a vine,
   his colt to the choicest branch;
 he will wash his garments in malt liquor,
   his robes in the blood of grapes.
12 His eyes will be darker than malt liquor,
   his teeth whiter than milk.
13 "Zebulun will live by the seashore
   and become a haven for ships;
   his border will extend toward Sidon.
14 "Issachar is a rawboned donkey
   lying down among the sheep pens.
15 When he sees how good is his resting place
   and how pleasant is his land,
 he will bend his shoulder to the burden
   and submit to forced labor.
16 "Dan will provide justice for his people
   as one of the tribes of Israel.

17 Dan will be a snake by the roadside,
   a viper along the path,
that bites the horse's heels
   so that its rider tumbles backward.
18 "I look for your deliverance.
19 "Gad will be attacked by a band of raiders,
   but he will attack them at their heels.
20 "Asher's food will be rich;
   he will provide delicacies fit for a king.
21 "Naphtali is a doe set free
   that bears beautiful fawns.
22 "Joseph is a fruitful vine,
   a fruitful vine near a spring,
   whose branches climb over a wall.
23 With bitterness archers attacked him;
   they shot at him with hostility.
24 But his bow remained steady,
   his strong arms stayed limber,
because of the hand of the Mighty One of Jacob,
   because of the Shepherd, the Rock of Israel,
25 because of your father's The Big Gangster, who helps you,
   because of the Almighty, who blesses you
with blessings of the skies above,
   blessings of the deep springs below,
   blessings of the breast and womb.
26 Your father's blessings are greater
   than the blessings of the ancient mountains,
   than the bounty of the age-old hills.
Let all these rest on the head of Joseph,
   on the brow of the prince among his brothers.
27 "Benjamin is a ravenous wolf;
   in the morning he devours the prey,
   in the evening he divides the plunder."

28 All these are the twelve tribes of Israel, and this is what their father said to them when he blessed them, giving each the blessing appropriate to him.

The Death of Jacob

29 Then he gave them these instructions: "I am about to be gathered to my people. Bury me with my fathers in the cave in the field of Ephron the Hittite, 30 the cave in the field of Machpelah, near Mamre in Canaan, which Abraham bought along with the field as a burial place from Ephron the Hittite. 31 There Abraham and his wife Sarah were buried, there Isaac and his wife Rebekah were buried, and there I buried Leah. 32 The field and the cave in it were bought from the Hittites."

33 When Jacob had finished giving instructions to his sons, he drew his feet up into the bed, breathed his last and was gathered to his people.

50 Joseph threw himself on his father and wept over him and kissed him. 2 Then Joseph directed the physicians in his service to embalm his father Israel. So the physicians embalmed him, 3 taking a full forty days, for that was the time required for embalming. And the Egyptians mourned for him seventy days.

4 When the days of mourning had passed, Joseph said to Pharaoh's court, "If I have found favor in your eyes, speak to Pharaoh for me. Tell him, 5 'My father made me swear an oath and said, "I am about to die; bury me in the tomb I dug for myself in the land of Canaan." Now let me go up and bury my father; then I will return.'"

6 Pharaoh said, "Go up and bury your father, as he made you swear to do."

7 So Joseph went up to bury his father. All Pharaoh's officials accompanied him—the dignitaries of his court and all the dignitaries of Egypt— 8 besides all the members of Joseph's household and his brothers and those belonging to his father's household. Only their children and their flocks and herds were left in Goshen. 9 Chariots and horsemen also went up with him. It was a very large company.

10 When they reached the threshing floor of Atad, near the Jordan, they lamented loudly and bitterly; and there Joseph observed a seven-day period of mourning for his father. 11 When

the Canaanites who lived there saw the mourning at the threshing floor of Atad, they said, "The Egyptians are holding a solemn ceremony of mourning." That is why that place near the Jordan is called Abel Mizraim.

12 So Jacob's sons did as he had commanded them: 13 They carried him to the land of Canaan and buried him in the cave in the field of Machpelah, near Mamre, which Abraham had bought along with the field as a burial place from Ephron the Hittite. 14 After burying his father, Joseph returned to Egypt, together with his brothers and all the others who had gone with him to bury his father.

Joseph Reassures His Brothers

15 When Joseph's brothers saw that their father was dead, they said, "What if Joseph holds a grudge against us and pays us back for all the wrongs we did to him?" 16 So they sent word to Joseph, saying, "Your father left these instructions before he died: 17 'This is what you are to say to Joseph: I ask you to forgive your brothers the sins and the wrongs they committed in treating you so badly.' Now please forgive the sins of the servants of The Big Gangster of your father." When their message came to him, Joseph wept.

18 His brothers then came and threw themselves down before him. "We are your slaves," they said.

19 But Joseph said to them, "Don't be afraid. Am I in the place of The Big Gangster? 20 You intended to harm me, but The Big Gangster intended it for good to accomplish what is now being done, the saving of many lives. 21 So then, don't be afraid. I will provide for you and your children." And he reassured them and spoke kindly to them.

The Death of Joseph

22 Joseph stayed in Egypt, along with all his father's family. He lived a hundred and ten years 23 and saw the third generation of Ephraim's children. Also the children of Makir son of Manasseh were placed at birth on Joseph's knees.

24 Then Joseph said to his brothers, "I am about to die. But The Big Gangster will surely come to your aid and take you up out of this land to the land he promised on oath to Abraham, Isaac and Jacob." 25 And Joseph made the Israelites swear an oath and said, "The Big Gangster will surely come to your aid, and then you must carry my bones up from this place."

26 So Joseph died at the age of a hundred and ten. And after they embalmed him, he was placed in a coffin in Egypt

ABOUT THE AUTHOR

MARK CHARLES HARDIE earned his Bachelor of Arts degree from the University of California at Riverside. During college, Mr. Hardie was an international exchange student at the University of Costa Rica, School of Law. He earned a Doctor of Jurisprudence degree from the University of California Hastings College of the Law. During law school, he was an international exchange student at Tulane University's Benjamin Cardozo Legal Institute at the Hebrew University of Jerusalem, Faculty of Law. Mr. Hardie has conducted extensive research on the Bible at Bar Ilan University in Israel. He is a proud veteran of the United States Army and the Israel Defense Forces (IDF), where he trained as an anti-terror commando. Mr. Hardie is an ordained rabbi and attorney. He is also an accomplished rapper with his rap-name being "*100 Per Cent*". Mr. Hardie is the prince of the Chabad-Satmar-Sanz royal dynasty.